GRAND THEFT CAPITAL

GRAND THEFT CAPITAL

What Workers Should Know about the Affordability Crisis

by FRED MAGDOFF *and* JOHN BELLAMY FOSTER

MONTHLY REVIEW PRESS
New York

Library of Congress Cataloging-in-Publication Data
available from the publisher.

978-1-68590-177-6 ISBN Paper
978-1-68590-178-3 ISBN Cloth

Typeset in Minion Pro and Bliss

MONTHLY REVIEW PRESS, NEW YORK
monthlyreview.org

5 4 3 2 1

Contents

Preface

This book originated with a 2023 article in *Monthly Review* titled "Grand Theft Capital: The Increasing Exploitation and Robbery of the U.S. Working Class." The book's central theme is that U.S. workers have been getting the short end of the stick for decades. They are struggling economically just to get by but do not understand who or what is responsible. At the same time wealthy Americans are becoming ever more fabulously rich. Those in power work to deflect blame on immigrants, minorities, or the supposed moral failings of workers—anywhere but on businesses, the wealthy, and the capitalist system itself as it functions in the United States.

The problem of working people being unable to afford a decent existence is not a new one. It also didn't happen overnight or by accident. It developed over decades as a result of the considerable efforts of the wealthy and corporations to become even wealthier—to accumulate ever more capital.

We would like to thank those who provided feedback on the manuscript during its development, especially Will Fritzmeier, Jim Roll, and Jan Schultz, and—in relation to the earlier article—John Mage, Brett Clark, Hannah Holleman, Intan Suwandi, R. Jamil

Jonna, and Victor Wallis. Jamil, especially, helped us with charts in both the article and book. We would also like to thank Michael Yates for his encouragement at all stages of this project.

—FRED MAGDOFF
BURLINGTON, VT

—JOHN BELLAMY FOSTER
EUGENE, OREGON

FEBRUARY 2, 2026

Introduction

> [Did] the relatively high inequality of the US and the insecurity of those in the bottom and middle of the income distribution inevitably lead to what I called "pluto-populism" . . . the political marriage of the ultra-rich, seeking deregulation and low taxes, with the insecure and angry middle and lower middle, seeking people to blame for what is going wrong for them[?] If so, what . . . in this age of deindustrialisation and unbridled finance, led to the rise of Trump and so to a shift to a dangerous new demagogic autocracy?
>
> —Martin Wolf, *Financial Times*, December 3, 2024

THE 2024 ELECTION, IN WHICH Donald Trump won a plurality of votes cast as well as a majority in the Electoral College, was not a fluke event. It follows a pattern of autocrats (including fascists) coming to power after the development of enormous levels of inequality. Many people, struggling to get by, become angry when they see the intellectual and economic "elites" having so much control over society and its wealth. During the Great Financial Crisis/

Great Recession* of 2007–2009 banks and corporations were bailed out while millions, unable to pay their mortgages, lost their homes. Thus, many people are dismayed and angry that their own situation appears static or getting worse while the wealthy become even richer. (Note: the Great Financial Crisis refers to the bursting of the financial bubble and the effects on financial assets while the Great Recession refers to the impact on the "real economy" as measured by GDP and employment.)

There are a number of significant explanations for Trump's win. These certainly include widespread misogyny and racism. Other reasons include the influx of cash and active support by Elon Musk and other billionaires and the silence of the frightened business owners and managers who have or desire contracts from the national government or fear the effects of being called out as "enemies" by Trump. The optics of the seemingly uncontrolled large number of immigrants coming across the southern border and the burdens it caused for communities trying to accommodate them was also a very potent factor (although Trump's opposition to congressional legislation to reduce the number caused it to fail, purposely maintaining immigration as a useful campaign issue). And it wasn't just the optics; it was estimated that for 2020–2023 there was a record two million new immigrants per year.[1] The discussion of the election and the failures of the Democratic Party will go on for some time.

---

*The Great Financial Crisis is usually seen as having started in August 2007 with the collapse of two Bear Stearns hedge funds. The Great Recession that resulted in the "real economy" is dated by the National Bureau of Economic Research as beginning in December 2007 and ending in June 2009. In the following analysis, we sometimes single out the Great Financial Crisis, when we are concerned mainly with the financial shock, and to the Great Recession, when the focus is on the real economy/GDP. But we frequently refer to them together since, although the Great Financial Crisis technically preceded the Great Recession by a number of months, and even though one points to the financial system and the other to GDP, they were in fact two parts of the same phenomenon.

WHAT IS NEOLIBERALISM?

Economic "liberalism" refers to the nineteenth-century promotion of free trade and *laissez-faire*, free from government regulations and interference. "Neoliberalism" is used to describe a modern version, pushing for loosening or eliminating barriers to free trade and capital movement among countries, decreased government regulations of all kinds (labor laws, environmental regulations, etc.), privatization of government functions, and low taxes on business and the wealthy. Under neoliberalism the state itself is to be run increasingly on a corporate basis. It thus points in an oligarchic direction. Let businesses and the wealthy keep more of their income and do what they want with their money. This will supposedly lead to a vibrant economy, so the fairy tale goes. Instead, neoliberalism increased economic and political power in the hands of capital while workers suffered stagnating incomes.

Possessive individualism has always been encouraged by capitalism. We are taught to compete with one another starting at an early age—for grades, in contests, in athletics, to get into the "right" school, and later for jobs. But a rampant individualism was stimulated by the neoliberal project. Promoters claimed that we are living in a "meritocracy" in which those who have more wealth deserve it because they are highly accomplished in education or business. This provides the "explanation" for why the rich deserve their money because they work so hard or are so smart. They should therefore keep as much of their wealth as possible to use as they see fit. The poor, on the other hand, have mostly themselves to blame—they are too lazy, didn't get a good education, made poor choices, and so on. One of the early promoters of neoliberalism, Britain's prime minister Margaret Thatcher, went as far as claiming that "There is no such thing" as a society (with obligations to help individuals). The existence and justification of this so-called meritocracy avoids the issue that people have very different opportunities beginning with the wealth and status of the family into which they are born.[2]

There are indications that lingering effects of the COVID-19 pandemic may have also contributed to Trump's win, as people believed they had moved past that period though still experiencing persistent anger and mental health issues. There has also been a reaction to the detrimental effects of the policies of the establishment: for years, politicians of both parties, as well as academics, provided theories and rationalizations for neoliberalism. Although in years past many workers believed the Democrats represented their interests, many now felt abandoned by the party. According to the president of the International Union of Painters and Allied Trades: "Every time we talk politics, the first thing that comes up is, 'The Democrats let us down.'"[3] There was so little difference between the Democratic and the Republican parties that the choice for many on the left was between Tweedledee and Tweedledum. Both parties have consistently favored the rich over the poor. Both parties have maintained an aggressive foreign policy, becoming involved in frequent wars, interventions, and assassinations abroad. There were a significant number of people who grew disenchanted with the U.S. forever wars abroad, costing many lives, both in the United States and more so in the foreign countries, and residual damage to the wounded.

Until Trump became president in 2017, both parties were in favor of the free trade agreements and organizations desired and designed by capital, such as NAFTA and the WTO. These encouraged production of goods overseas and a continuing hollowing out of a significant portion of U.S. manufacturing communities. Both parties allowed the continued growth of monopolies/oligopolies as antitrust enforcement declined (with the exception of Biden's 2021 appointment of Lina Khan as chair of the Federal Trade Commission, reversed by Trump). There has been a push toward privatization of public functions such as water and wastewater utilities, electricity, prisons, and education.

The commonly used economic indicators suggested that the U.S. economy was doing relatively well in 2024. The official unemployment rate was low at around 4 percent and national income as measured by the GDP was growing at 2.8 percent a year. The overall rate of inflation had declined significantly from a sharp but short burst that began as supply chains were disrupted during the depths of the COVID-19 pandemic. Construction was increasing, and new factories were going up. Although the COVID-19 era stimulus/rescue laws were ending, a whole new set of Biden-era stimulus laws such as the Inflation Reduction Act, Infrastructure Investment and Jobs Act, and the CHIPS and Science Act were coming into effect. How could it be that the economy was the top issue on voters' minds during the election of Trump to a second term?

While the more affluent were spending liberally as their stock market portfolios inflated, many were left behind after the pandemic, even though there was a significant amount of funding to help. People had been kept afloat during the pandemic by increased government spending, including checks sent to individual households, and the expansion of the Child Tax Credit, helping to reduce the effects of the short recession on the population in general. Homelessness and hunger, which had decreased during the pandemic, returned to pre-pandemic levels or worse when social support funding ran out. About 640 counties in the United States, with a population of 30 million, did not return to their pre-COVID-19 level of economic output. Trump won 570 (almost 90 percent) of those counties.[4] Even in other locations across the country, the combination of inadequate pay raises and the increased costs, especially for food and shelter, created discontent. According to a survey by the Department of Housing and Urban Development in January 2024 the numbers of U.S. homeless stood at an estimated 771,000, an 18 percent increase over 2023. But when those who are not out on the streets or in shelters—living in cars, recreational vehicles, or with friends or family, many with low-paying jobs—are included in the estimate, the total number of homeless may well be over 4 million.[5]

Political partisanship prior to the election plus looking mainly at large-scale data helps to explain the upbeat descriptions of the economy based on national economic statistics—for example, "Bidenomics Is Still Working Very Well" according to Paul Krugman,[6] "How good is the U.S. economy? It's beating pre-pandemic predictions" by Catherine Rampell,[7] and Dean Baker commented that "the economic picture under Biden actually looks great."[8]

Nevertheless, the working population, as the 2024 elections confirmed, remained distressed about the economy. A considerable portion was in trouble and having a hard time making ends meet and were very concerned about their future. A study of how Americans across the country viewed the economy over the previous two years found:

> While national indicators may suggest that the economy is strong, the Americans we listened to are mostly not thriving. They do not see the economy as nourishing or supporting them. Instead, they tend to see it as an obstacle, a set of external forces out of their control that nonetheless seems to hold sway over their lives.
>
> Take the perceived prevalence of greed. This is hardly a new feeling, but it has been exacerbated recently by inflation and higher housing costs. Americans experience these phenomena not as abstract concepts or political talking points but rather as grocery stores and landlords demanding more money.[9]

In other words, many people "believe the rich and powerful have designed the economy to benefit themselves and have left others with too little or with nothing at all."[10]

In fact, this belief is absolutely correct—*the system is rigged!* And it did not get that way by accident. Rather, the way society functions today is the result of a decades-long concerted and multipronged effort on the part of the wealthy and corporations to accumulate more capital.

The purpose of capitalist business is, of course, to make profits, and that of the wealthy to amass ever greater amounts of wealth. By employing the labor power of workers to use raw materials/parts and tools/machines, commodities are produced and sold for more than it cost to produce them. This is the source of profits in the production of goods and services. For most capitalists there is no such thing as *enough profit*—their greed and the normal way the system works propel a continual drive to greater accumulation of wealth. And economic power—especially when concentrated into fewer and fewer hands—leads to political power. It should not be a surprise that taxes on the wealthy and corporations have decreased and that the decades-long attack on labor unions has been successful.[11]

Workers are not happy about their working conditions. According to a Gallup survey, "Only one-third of respondents said they are engaged at their jobs, while half are giving minimum effort—dubbed as 'quiet quitting.'"[12] In fact, 34 percent of workers surveyed in 2023 often dreaded to go to work because general job satisfaction has tumbled.[13] Many are paid so little per week that they need to work multiple jobs, leaving them exhausted, with less time to spend with family and friends. And even in the tech industry, extravagant perks are mostly gone and people are being asked to work harder. No wonder, according to the title of a *Wall Street Journal* article, even tech workers "Are Just Like the Rest of Us: Miserable at Work."[14]

At the same time that many are dissatisfied with their work, housing has become extremely expensive relative to incomes, and the burst of inflation has affected other basic costs as well. Altogether, food prices rose by 26 percent between 2020 and 2025, housing by 27 percent, and transportation costs by 36 percent.[15] Therefore, when the gauges commonly used to evaluate the health of a capitalist economy such as growth of the gross domestic product (GDP) and the unemployment rate seem to indicate that the *economy* is doing well, they *do not* indicate how well *workers* are doing. And while there were significant wage increases for low-income jobs for a few years following the pandemic, it is understandable that many people are finding it difficult to make ends meet when prices rise so rapidly. Real wages (the purchasing power after accounting for inflation) of workers remain stuck at what they received a half-century ago, while capital's expropriation by various means of workers' streams of income has increased.[16]

These and other pressures on working people, plus a severely inadequate and costly health system, have serious consequences, not only on people's day-to-day lives but also on longevity. Compared to other countries, the U.S. rankings in social progress indicators have declined. Its overall rank regarding the social indicators in 2026 is 32 out of 171 countries. And with regard to meeting the population's basic needs it ranks 51st and for safety it ranks 99th.[17] The head of the organization that publishes the social progress index explained: "It's not about Trump. Obama and Biden did little to reverse the decline, nor did the Bushes or Clinton. It's a multipresident, bipartisan, long, slow car crash. Yet voters seem to have been anesthetized by a rising stock market and economic growth, until in recent years it's become clear to people that their living standards have stagnated."[18]

These developments have caused life expectancy in the United States to be significantly below that in comparable countries. In 1980 life expectancy in the United States was 73.7 years, close to the 74.5 years for comparable countries. But by 2022, life expectancy in the United States was 77.5 years while it was 82.2 years in comparable countries.[19] Compared to other high-income countries, the United States is in 33rd place for the child death, suicide, and murder rates, 10th in social isolation, 7th in trust in other people, and 8th in voter participation.[20] And a Pentagon study found that "more than three-quarters of Americans between the ages of seventeen and twenty-four are ineligible for military service, because they are overweight, unable to pass the aptitude test, afflicted by physical or mental-health issues, or disqualified by such factors as a criminal record."[21]

Many point to supposed U.S. "exceptionalism," according to which it is not only different from other countries but also somehow better and even exemplary. However, the United States *is* truly exceptional in the harm done to its environment, in its propensity to go to war abroad, and in the poor economic and social conditions of its people compared to other wealthy countries.

From the Beginning

Capitalism has always been based on the theft of land, resources, and human lives in order to create the conditions for the exploitation of labor. The Industrial Revolution was made possible by means of the brutal enclosure of the commons in England together with the even more barbaric colonization abroad carried out by the European powers, encompassing "the discovery of gold and silver in the Americas, the extirpation, enslavement, and entombment in mines of the indigenous population" of those continents and "the beginnings of the conquest and plunder of India." This also included the hunting, capturing, transporting, and enslaving of Africans to work in the plantations of the Caribbean, Brazil, and the United States. Taken together, these forms of "original expropriation" formed the historical basis for the "genesis of the industrial capitalist."[22]

The development of the textile industry, manufacturing the first mass-produced commodity, was supported by slavery. As historian Walter Johnson explains:

> In the years before the Civil War, there was no capitalism without slavery. The two were, in many ways, one and the same. . . . It is not simply that the labor of enslaved people underwrote 19th-century capitalism. Enslaved people were the capital: four million people worth at least $3 billion in 1860, which was more than all the capital invested in railroads and factories in the United States combined. Seen in this light, the

> conventional distinction between slavery and capitalism fades into meaninglessness.[23]

From the sixteenth and seventeenth centuries to the present day, capitalists have plundered natural as well as human resources with abandon, squandering fresh water, soil, forests, fisheries, and mineral deposits. The world has become a sink in which to pour industrial wastes using the cheapest form of disposal. Today's planetary ecological crisis is a direct result of this plundering and pollution of the earth.[24]

Capital and Labor in Capitalist Economies

Although outright *expropriation* (robbery) is always present in capitalism, the inner dynamic of the system arises from the *exploitation* of labor power, a more hidden form of robbery. The wealthy, most establishment economists, and much of the general public view the wages earned by workers from their employers to be the result of a completely rational and fair process. Enshrined in the entire legal system, this way of thinking assumes these relations are based simply on an equal exchange. After all, workers are free to take a job with a given wage and benefits (if any) or not. For their part, capitalists will only employ workers when they can make a profit doing so. The relationship between boss and workers commonly appears as one of "equality," as if it were a transparent contract mutually agreed upon with equal power on both sides. But behind this appearance of rational and freely made decisions based on equal exchange lies a very different reality.

Workers producing goods and services add greater value to products than the value of the wages they are paid. Part of every working day is necessarily devoted to reproducing the *value of labor power* as measured by the wages paid to the workers. The remainder of the working day is dedicated to producing *surplus value* (gross profits) for the owners of the means of production. Capitalists therefore have a direct interest in increasing the *rate of exploitation* of the workers by increasing the portion of the working day devoted to producing surplus value and decreasing the portion devoted to the reproduction of the labor power of the workers. Surplus value appropriated by the capitalists in this way forms the basis of capital accumulation, directly enhancing the power and wealth of the capitalist class in relation to the working class.

The general relations between labor and capital are far from equal, with capital in a very strong position compared to most workers. The capitalist owns the land, the place of business, the machinery, the money used in the running of the business, and the jobs. The workers own little or nothing but their capacity to work, which they can sell but usually under conditions not of their own choosing. A significant disadvantage that most workers face is that they are not able to make a living on their own, lacking the money capital, tools, and facilities with which to engage in production. Starting a small business is rarely a viable option due to a lack of capital or difficult competition. Certain types of businesses are now nearly impossible to start with high costs to begin with and competition from monopolies such as Walmart and Amazon. Approximately 20 percent of new businesses fail in the first year, and 65 percent fail in the first ten years.[25] Most of the successful ones tend to be absorbed by bigger companies. Thus, workers are generally forced to take jobs where and when they can find them.

Workers are typically subjected to a labor process determined entirely by the owners. It is the boss who sets conditions of work and defines what is expected from workers. Moreover, it is the business owner who has the power to hire and fire, with little in the way of contractual relations preventing the worker from being made "redundant" and laid off. Elizabeth Anderson, professor of philosophy and women's studies at the University of Michigan, explains: "When we are workers, we lie under the government of a boss. It's a dictatorship. The boss rules."[26] Much of labor is in a precarious situation, not knowing if a round of firings might occur when economic downturns strike, if a decision will be made to outsource the work or produce in another region or another country, or if the boss might simply take a dislike to an individual worker, who would then be "let go." In addition, the precarious nature of work has been fueled by the rise of gig workers who face constantly changing schedules and hours of work per week, and by the uncertainties and inequities of part-time and temporary work. These issues go even deeper, as described by someone who has worked in a big box store:

> Part-time work today also has a particular predatory logic, shifting economic risk from employers to employees. And because part-time work has become so ubiquitous in certain predominantly low-wage sectors of the economy, many workers are unable to find full-time alternatives. They end up trapped in jobs that don't pay enough to live on and aren't predictable enough to plan a life around.[27]

"Right to work" laws—which allow nonunion members to opt out of paying dues to a union that represents their interests—have been put into place in many states following lobbying campaigns by capital and have served to weaken unions and protection for workers.[28] Three states—North Carolina, South Carolina, and Utah—have outlawed collective bargaining for all public employees while Texas allows only police and fire fighters to do so.[29]

Today's Affordability Crisis

The affordability crisis played a significant role in Trump's 2024 election campaign, where he promised to bring prices down, and the debate continues among politicians in 2026. While affordability concerns have existed for decades, the rapid inflation burst of 2021–2023 intensified the problem considerably.

In a *Washington Post* opinion piece, author and investor Zachary Karabell explains the long-term nature of the problem:

> What is clear over the past 30 to 40 years is that more people are feeling less secure. It is also clear that the economic system has consistently failed to work for tens of millions of Americans. That is a failure of a vastly affluent society that generates mind-boggling wealth for the top tier of society. Over this same period, and notably emerging with the dot-com bubble of the 1990s and the rise in the compensation of corporate executives and Wall Street managers, the upper tier has benefited disproportionately.[30]

The important question is why has the economic system consistently failed to work for tens of millions of Americans, leaving so many feeling less secure? Although other issues exist, the failures result primarily from two interconnected factors: rising prices and wages that fail to keep pace with those increases. But how can it be that incomes for many workers stagnate while there is an accumulation of "mind-boggling wealth for the top tier of society"?

The most straightforward answer is expropriation or robbery. To steal someone else's car by larceny deception, or trickery, is considered a crime—grand theft auto. But when capitalists rob working people of their livelihood no one goes to jail. *Grand Theft Capital* is the story of the many ways in which this vast expropriation is taking place in the United States today, creating a widespread affordability crisis, and the need to reverse this process—to expropriate the expropriators.

1

Overview of U.S. Workers

BASED ON THE DECEMBER 2025 jobs report, there were at the time about 171 million people in the U.S. workforce (civilian, non-institutional population, including the officially unemployed). Around 164 million people were employed in one capacity or another, including part-time and contract workers. About 7.5 million people were officially classified as unemployed, meaning that they were actively looking for work (Table 1.1). Another 6.4 million people indicated through the employment surveys that they "want a job now," but were not included in the labor force (or the unemployed) as they did not report that they had looked for a job recently. More than a quarter of those 6.4 million were classified as "marginally attached," including those designated as "discouraged," having not looked for work in the last four weeks. (Many of the marginally attached were blocked from seeking employment by structural obstacles, such as lack of childcare or adequate transportation.) The remainder of the 6.4 million who indicated they "want a job now"—and who were not listed as marginally attached (or discourged)—either had not searched for work in the last year or remained uncategorized due to lack of detailed information. In addition, more than 4.3 million workers were employed in part-time jobs but wanted full-time employment.

The December 2025 official unemployment rates were low by historical standards, at 4.4 percent, mainly due to a steep decline in the labor participation rate, that is, those participating in the labor market as either employed or officially unemployed. However, if all of those "wanting a job now" but not officially considered in the labor force or unemployed are added in, along with part-time workers wanting full-time employment, the *real* as opposed to the *official* ("U-3") unemployment rate would be around 10 percent (see Table 1.1 and Figure 1.1). The number of people who are not working but desire employment is therefore more than double those classified as officially "unemployed."

About 24 million workers are government employees: 3 million employed by the federal government (excluding the military) and 21 million employed by state and local governments. Most jobs are in the private sector, representing approximately 85 percent of workers. Less than 2 percent of civilian workers are federal government employees while local and state governments employ about 13 percent.

One important distinction in labor statistics is the separation

Table 1.1. U.S. Workforce Overview, December 2025

	Number of Workers (Millions)
A. Officially Employed (CE16OV)	164*
B. Officially Unemployed (UNEMP)	7.5
Official Civilian Labor Force	**171.5****
C. Those who "want a job now" but not classifed as part of the labor force (includes 1.75 million workers classified as "marginally attached" or discouraged)	6.4

Sources and Notes: Bureau of Labor, "The Employment Situation–August 2025," Kaitlyn Hoevelmann, "The Labor Force Participation Rate Explained," St. Louis Fed, May 5, 2023. About one-fifth of the workforce is foreign born.

* Includes 4.3 million part-time workers wanting full employment.

** Excludes those in category C below.

Figure 1.1: Real Unemployment, 1994-2005

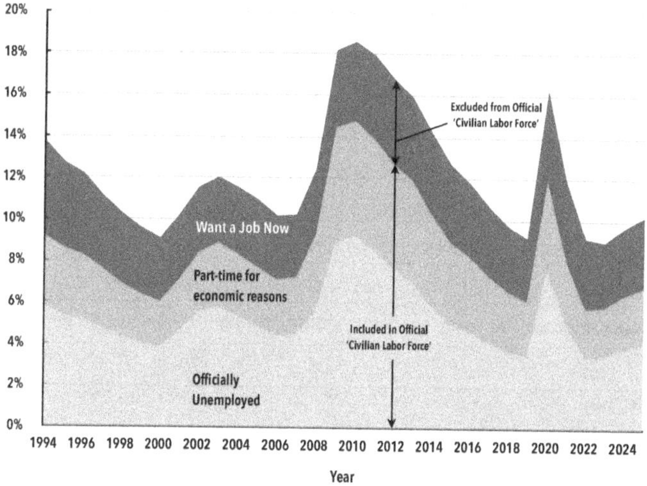

Sources and Notes: Data is from the following series: Federal Reserve Economic Data (FRED), Federal Reserve Bank of St. Louis: Series *CLF16OV*, "Civilian Labor Force Level, Thou-sands of Persons, Monthly, Seasonally Adjusted"; series *UNEMPLOY*, "Unemployment Level, Thousands of Persons, Monthly, Seasonally Adjusted"; series *LNS12032194*, "Employment Level - Part-Time for Economic Reasons, All Industries, Thousands of Persons, Monthly, Seasonally Adjusted"; and series *NILFWJN*, "Not in Labor Force–Want a Job Now, Thousands of Persons, Monthly, Seasonally Adjusted." Calculated by dividing each series by Civilian Labor Force (CLF16OV) + Want a Job Now (NILFWJN).

of "production and non-supervisory" workers from the total 163 million employed. Production and non-supervisory workers consistently represent over 80 percent of workers in private businesses.

Slowdown in Growth of the Labor Force

Following the entry of post–Second World War baby boomers into the workforce, the rate of growth in the size of the workforce slowed considerably. Peak growth was 2.7 percent annually in the 1970s, followed by steady declines to an annual 0.6 percent increase from 2010 to 2024 (Figure 1.2). Although the number of U.S.-born workers was about the same in 2024 as before the

EXPLOITATION OF INCARCERATED WORKERS

People in U.S. prisons and jails are not counted as part of the labor force. But the authority of governments to force incarcerated people to work is spelled out in the U.S. Constitution's Thirteenth Amendment: "Neither slavery nor involuntary servitude, except as a punishment for crime whereof the party shall have been duly convicted, shall exist within the United States, or any place subject to their jurisdiction."[1] Although not part of the "official" workforce, most people in jails and prisons are required to work and may be sent to solitary confinement if they refuse. They earn incredibly low wages (less than a dollar an hour). The approximately two million people in jails and prisons are estimated to produce commodities worth more than 2 billion dollars and produce services worth 9 billion dollars in the prisons in which they are held.[2]

DISABLED WORKERS ALSO EXPLOITED

Since the 1930s it has been legal to pay disabled workers below the federal minimum wage, currently $7.50 an hour. In 2019–2021 half of disabled workers were estimated to be paid less than $3.50 an hour and many earn $1 dollar an hour or less.[3]

pandemic, there were approximately 2.9 million more foreign-born workers in the United States in 2023 than in 2019. This helps to explain the easing of the labor market following the relatively tight conditions as the economy began to recover from the effects of the COVID-19 pandemic.

The Importance of Immigrant Workers

For the last half-century, with the exception of 2006 and 2007, the U.S. birthrate has been below the replacement rate of 2.1 children per woman, standing at 1.6 in 2024.[4] In spite of this, the natural population level (births minus deaths) continued to increase

Figure 1.2: Annual Percent Change in U.S. Labor Force

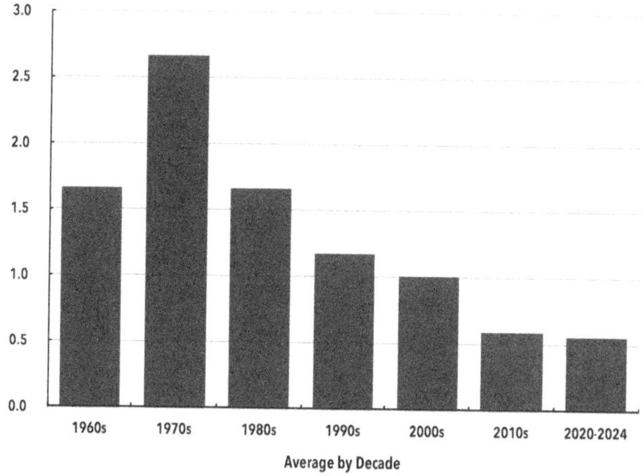

Sources and Notes: FRED, Series CLF16OV, "Civilian Labor Force Level, Percent Change from Year Ago of (Thousands of Persons), Annual, Seasonally Adjusted." Data Updated: 2026-01-09. Presented as the average for each decade.

slowly. But the continual growth of the economy—a necessary feature of capitalism—requires an ever-increasing number of workers, more than this low natural increase. Thus, immigrant labor, historically important to the U.S. economy, remains critical today. In the summer of 2024 (prior to the advent of the second Trump administration with its extreme deportation policies), there were 32 million foreign-born workers in the labor force, both employed and unemployed, representing nearly one-fifth of total workers. And although there is a strong anti-immigrant strain within the right, business interests are well aware of the importance of continuing immigration in order to have an adequate labor supply.

Although a system is in place to allow highly skilled works to enter the United States, there is no such system for the long-term workers from abroad needed to fill many low-skilled and low-pay jobs: in eldercare, slaughterhouses and meat processing plants, construction, roofing, janitorial, hospitality, etc. (There is a program for using short-term labor, H2A for agricultural workers and H2B for others). But asylum seekers that have filed the proper forms are able to receive work permits six months later. Combined with a real need for labor, this has created the supply of workers to fill the gap. While Republican politicians rail against immigrants, a North Dakota state senator commented, "I summarize the whole thing in six words. We need them. They need us."[5]

With about half of all workers added to the labor force from 2007 through 2024 born abroad, the importance of immigration to help fill job openings at this particular time is clear. Close to 16 percent of the U.S. population was born in another country—"even after taking into account today's larger U.S. population, the recent surge [of immigrants, 2021–2023] is the most rapid since at least 1850."[6] While the need for immigrant labor should be part of any discussion of immigration, it is mostly omitted. Immigrants are essential to a capitalist economy in which the number of native-born workers is either not growing or in actual decline. Thus, the massive deportations of foreign-born workers under the current Trump administration spells significant labor shortages in key areas such as construction, farming, food processing, healthcare and so on.

Just How Good Are Today's "Well-Paying Jobs" in Manufacturing?

Politicians talk about "bringing back" well-paying manufacturing jobs. But how "well-paying" are these jobs? Manufacturing jobs in 2025 paid about 7 percent less per hour than the average hourly pay for all private sector workers. But because workers in manufacturing do more hours than the average private worker, their weekly income is higher. Hourly pay in manufacturing and service industries is about the same.[7] So why do politicians proclaim that they will "bring back" "good-paying industrial" jobs to the United States? They are remembering a now distant past when manufacturing industries were heavily unionized—when labor's bargaining power affected even workers in nonunion shops. That is no longer so.

While it is certainly better to have a strong union, many manufacturing jobs, even in unionized workplaces, are not able to provide the standard of living they once did. Not only have the wages of manufacturing workers stagnated, but levels of employment and job security have decreased. Pensions and other benefits have eroded. The wage premium that manufacturing workers once received, relative to workers in general, has declined.[8] In the fall of 2024, 96 percent of Boeing workers, members of the International Association of Machinists and Aerospace Workers, voted to strike. Their situation provides examples of the issues. "Ariel McKenzie recalls that it was a big deal when her father landed a job at Boeing 20 years ago. So, when he suggested she also join the company, it seemed like a smart move: Working at the company had given her dad and the other Boeing long-timers a good life, paying for roomy houses, nice trucks, motorbikes and vacations. But after a decade making aircraft parts at a factory in Auburn, Wash., McKenzie, 35, said the job hasn't given her the same financial boost."[9]

Companies struggling during and after the Great Financial Crisis/Great Recession of 2007–2009 put pressure on unions to "give back" benefits and agree to lower wage scales. While politicians talk about bringing back so-called well-paying union jobs, even many unionized workers in manufacturing are not doing as well as former generations.

> Generations of workers coveted Boeing jobs in the Seattle area, where the company was founded over a century ago and helped usher in the age of global air travel. Going to work in its cavernous factories promised economic security and the pride of working on the world's most iconic planes: the ubiquitous 737, the giant 747 Jumbo Jet and the high-tech 787 Dreamliner. The

economic benefits passed down within families, as children and grandchildren landed jobs with the aerospace giant.[10]

Types of Jobs Are Changing

The structure of jobs in the economy has changed dramatically since the end of the Second World War. The percent of workers in direct farming activities continued its long decline so that now only 1 percent work in that sector. Employment in manufacturing, about one-third of all private workers in 1960, declined continuously until reaching a plateau following the 2007–2009 Great Financial Crisis. In 2024, around 8 percent of the private workforce was in manufacturing. At the same time, labor in the service sector increased steadily so that it now represents close to 80 percent of workers. A combination of factors led this to happen, such as multinational corporations exporting jobs to countries with lower unit labor costs, greater import of goods, and the natural shift to purchasing more services as a society becomes wealthier. However, the increased labor efficiency from automation (robotization) explains a significant portion of the loss of manufacturing jobs.[11]

Although politicians still refer to increasing the number of "good-paying manufacturing jobs," the reality is that manufacturing jobs have been declining for decades. Although the United States is only relatively deindustrialized as compared with the mid-twentieth century and still has considerable industrial power, the loss of a significant number of industrial plants has been harmful for communities and workers. Manufacturing as a whole currently produces more goods—real value (corrected for inflation)—than in the late 1990s and about as much as in 2005 before the Great Financial Crisis, but with 30 percent less labor and only using about 75 to 80 percent capacity. U.S. industry still produces a lot of steel, amounting to 79.5 million metric tons (in 2024), about two-thirds the peak production years of the early 1970s. U.S. steel imports, at 26 metric tons in 2024, were less than half of the amount produced internally. The largest effect on the number of workers in the industry came from the change in technology used, drastically *decreasing* labor needed to produce a ton of steel, from around 10 hours in 1980 to less than 2 hours today, and with electric arc mills (minimills) needing about 0.5 labor hours per ton.[12] Manufacturing labor productivity (real value of output per hour) more than doubled from the 1980s until the start of the Great Recession (2007–2009), but has changed little since then. Output (in value) per hour for all of manufacturing increased by two and a half times between the 1980s and 2010. Summarizing the causes for the employment decline in goods production, economists Kehoe, Ruhl, and Steinberg found that "only 15.1 percent of the decline in goods-sector employment from 1992 to 2012 stems from US trade deficits; most of the decline is due to differential productivity growth."[13] The "automation shock" was quite a bit larger than the "China shock." Manufacturing employment, after recovering to about 13 million workers after the disruption of the COVID-19 pandemic, has decreased by about 300,000 workers between 2022 and December 2025.

The reality is that with automation and recently the combination of robots and artificial intelligence (AI), fewer workers are needed to produce or distribute a given amount of stuff. In July 2025, Amazon was "on the cusp" of having more robots than workers at its large distribution sites.[14]

The United States *is* importing a larger *percentage* of manufacturing goods sold in the country than in the past. However, because of the drastic rise in automation (robots and AI) plus the many areas of production that will not be returning to the United States, the chances of major increases in manufacturing employment are quite small, Trump's tariffs notwithstanding.

A survey of millions of college graduates over the decade of 2012–2021 found that over half had jobs that did not require a college degree.[15] The job market when graduating and what kind of job one has a year later have profound effects on whether the graduate is unemployed/underemployed a decade later. And with the huge degree of uncertainty surrounding the economy and society in 2025, college graduates are in an especially difficult job market. Thus, conditions that people have no control over have significant effects on their future work trajectory.

While automation has already had a profound effect on the numbers of workers needed for production, it is not clear how the continued introduction of AI into the economy combined with advances in robotics will play out. Much of the work in training the AI algorithms is done abroad by low-paid labor. Google hired 100,000 temporary and contract workers to scan books at a rapid pace in time with a rhythm-regulated soundtrack as part of its plan to digitalize all of the world's books (estimated to be 130 million unique volumes). Although the project has been largely discontinued, it was regarded as a means of developing generative AI.[16] The expansion of AI has the potential to change the way work is conducted as well as eliminate many jobs, both blue- and white-collar, while creating more uncertain working conditions. Online surveys of the national workforce carried out by business groups such as McKinsey Global Institute "indicate [that] between 25 and 35 percent of workers" in the United States have "engaged in non-standard or gig work on a supplementary *or* primary basis in the preceding month. As of 2024, that means at least 41 million people in the United States are engaged in some form of gig work," usually as contingent workers. A major form of gig work today is "platform work," or employment arangements involving online platforms or mobile apps.

Although countless jobs are threatened by digitalization, much work in 2024 was not so much displaced overall as made more contingent and precarious.[17] But the effects on workers are changing rapidly. Amazon has increased its production dramatically through the use of robots, AI, and digitalization in general, and massive speedups enforced by enhanced surveillance, increasing daily packages shipped per worker from 175 in 2015 to 3,870 in 2025.[18] Many corporate CEOs—from Ford, JPMorgan Chase, Amazon, Anthropic—are saying that the new high technology will soon eliminate many jobs. And the CEO of Fiverr, a freelance marketplace, wrote: "It does not matter if you are a programmer, designer, product manager, data scientist, lawyer, customer support rep, salesperson, or a finance person—AI is coming for you."[19]

According to the IMF, the international lender of last resort, "about 60% of jobs in advanced economies such as the US and UK are exposed to AI and half of these jobs may be negatively affected."[20] In early 2024, it became clear that AI was already starting to significantly threaten white-collar jobs.[21] This is indicated by both the firing of current employees and the reduction in future job openings as companies grow. In early 2025 it was noted that "Deep Research from ChatGPT is capable of doing a lot of entry-level work that past generations of interns, analysts and computer programmers did. And this is only the beginning."[22]

Organized labor is very concerned about the possibilities of AI displacing many jobs—"The AFL-CIO and other labor groups are working with state legislators across the nation to advance AI regulations designed to protect workers."[23] The issue has become even more important after Trump did away with Biden-era rules, giving tech companies a free rein. As a *Washington Post* headline indicated: "Silicon Valley's bet on Trump starts to pay off."[24] Without significant government regulation, AI companies can operate freely, doing what is best for profits.

Only a few years into the AI era workers are deeply concerned that the new wave of high-tech automation will replace their jobs:

> At Chicago recruiting firm Hirewell, marketing agency clients have all but stopped requesting entry-level staff—young grads once in high demand but whose work is now a "home run" for AI, the firm's chief growth officer said. Dating app Grindr is hiring more seasoned engineers, forgoing some junior coders

straight out of school, and CEO George Arison said companies are "going to need less and less people at the bottom."[25]

Anthropic, one of the main companies providing AI tools to companies, has found:

> More than three quarters (77%) of companies' usage of Anthropic's Claude AI software involved automation patterns, often including "full task delegation," according to a research report the startup released on Monday. The finding was based on an analysis of traffic from Anthropic's application programming interface, which is used by developers and businesses.[26]

Because of the uncertainties and costs of the numerous upheavals in 2025, especially the effects of the unstable but expensive tariff environment, companies are using new ways to fatten their bottom lines. Many have decreased the number of middle managers, meaning that more people report to the remaining managers. Even if sales income decreases, profits can still increase because of fewer workers. As the chief financial officer of one company put it: "The outcome of those transformations means less head count, more productivity."[27]

Although there are serious problems common to all workers, the extent of the problems may differ between groups. Black workers represent about 13 percent of the workforce while white workers are about 76 percent, and Asian workers 7 percent. The remaining workers are American Indians, Alaskan Natives, Native Hawaiians, other Pacific Islanders, and people who are of two or more "racial" lineages. (People of Latinx or Hispanic ethnicity—as distinct from race—make up 19 percent of the labor force.)[28] In good times and bad, Black workers are unemployed at rates averaging about twice as high as white workers.

Slowdown in Job Openings and Increasingly Stubborn Unemployment

Job openings and new hires steadily dropped from a peak following the pandemic through the end of 2025 (although official data stopped because of the government shutdown). In August 2025 new hires were at a rate about the same as 2016, partway through the recovery from the Great Recession/Great Financial Crisis of 2007–2009. And although the rate of unemployment remained relatively low in 2025 and early 2026, about 25 percent of the unemployed were without jobs for more than six months. Low numbers of job openings and relatively high long-term unemployment indicate significant problems in the system.

Women Workers

The participation of women in workforce increased dramatically over the decades. Women, working in order to support themselves and their families, now account for nearly half of the U.S. workforce, compared with about one-third in the 1960s. While they represent nearly two-thirds of part-time workers (those working 0–34 hours per week), women make up just 45 percent of full-time wage and salary employees and, on average, earn nearly 20 percent less than their male counterparts.[29] Women also tend to be more concentrated in lower-paying "female" jobs such as health care, social services, and education.[30]

Although conditions for women in the workforce have improved significantly and women now represent well over half of college graduates, many problems remain in the workplace and at home. Women continue to spend considerably more time than men performing unpaid labor, including housework, childcare, and elder care. These responsibilities can negatively affect their earnings and career advancement.

The conditions faced by Black women workers are even more challenging than those experienced by white women. Black women remain significantly underrepresented in professional occupations, as highlighted by a *Wall Street Journal* headline: "40% of Lawyers Are Women. Only 7% Are Black."[31] The second Trump administration's attacks on workplace diversity, equity, and inclusion (DEI) initiatives, combined with large-scale layoffs of government employees, have had a particularly damaging impact on women workers overall—and an even more severe effect on Black women.[32]

2

The U.S. Ruling Class

FOR MORE THAN A CENTURY U.S. capitalism has been led by one of the world's most powerful and self-aware ruling classes—straddling both the economy and the state, and projecting its dominance at home and abroad. A central pillar of its power has been an ideological apparatus which insists that the extraordinary economic might of the capitalist class does not translate into control over the functioning of government. According to this narrative, even as economic inequality deepens, U.S. democracy remains unshaken because the market's rulers supposedly do not govern the country. This separation of economic and political power is treated as essential to liberal democracy. Yet this reigning ideology is rapidly eroding in the face of the structural crisis of U.S. and global capitalism and the decline of the liberal-democratic state itself. The result is widening fractures within the ruling class and the rise of a new, openly capitalist, right-wing domination of the state.

Trump's second ascent to the presidency does not signal the sudden emergence of capitalist oligarchs as decisive political actors; their influence has been entrenched for decades. (Capital's long-term offensive against labor, and its drive for lower taxes and weaker regulations, are discussed in chapters 5 and 6.)

Nevertheless, the political climate since the 2008 collapse of Lehman Brothers has shifted sharply to the right, and the oligarchy is now exerting more direct control over state power. A segment of the U.S. capitalist class is openly steering the ideological-state apparatus under a neofascist administration, with the old neoliberal establishment reduced to a subordinate role. The purpose of this transformation—while maintaining pressure on labor and creating new avenues for corporate and personal enrichment—is to reorganize the United States along more regressive lines and to maintain a permanent war footing. This shift reflects the erosion of U.S. global hegemony, the volatility of U.S. capitalism, and the need of an increasingly concentrated capitalist class to tighten its command over the state.

In the Cold War decades after the Second World War, defenders of the liberal-democratic order in universities and the media worked to downplay the dominant role of industrial and financial owners in the U.S. economy. They promoted the idea that a "managerial revolution" had displaced the traditional capitalist class, or that "countervailing power" had significantly constrained it. In this narrative, owners and managers, capital and labor, each exert limits on the other. A later variation dissolved the notion of a hegemonic capitalist class under monopoly capitalism into the hazy notion of "the corporate rich."[1]

According to this prevailing ideology, U.S. democracy was the outcome of competition among diverse social groups, or at times guided by a relatively small group described as "the power elite." But there was supposedly no coherent ruling class with dominance over both economic and political life. Even if a capitalist class could be said to rule the economy, it did not rule the state, which was assumed to possess independence from it. This message appeared across a wide ideological range—from James Burnham's *The Managerial Revolution* (1941) and Joseph

A. Schumpeter's *Capitalism, Socialism, and Democracy* (1942) to Robert Dahl's *Who Governs?* (1961) and John Kenneth Galbraith's *The New Industrial State* (1967). Though differing in emphasis, all these works advanced the same basic claim: U.S. politics was governed by pluralism or by technocratic managers, not by a capitalist class directing both the economy and the state. In this account—best articulated by Schumpeter—politicians acted as "political entrepreneurs" competing for votes just as firms compete for customers in the so-called free market, resulting in a system of "competitive leadership."[2]

This ideological framework, which upheld the fiction that the United States remained a genuine democracy despite the enormous power of the capitalist class, was further reinforced—ironically—by some thinkers on the left. The most influential example was C. Wright Mills's *The Power Elite* (1956). Mills argued that the Marxist conception of a ruling class should be replaced with a "power elite" composed of corporate leaders, military chiefs, and top elected politicians. He dismissed the ruling-class concept as a "short-cut theory" that too easily equated economic domination with political control. "The American government," Mills insisted, "is not, in any simple way nor as a structural fact, a committee of 'the ruling class.' It is a network of committees, and other men from other hierarchies besides the corporate rich sit in these committees."[3]

Mills's interpretation was contested by radical theorists—most notably Paul M. Sweezy in *Monthly Review* and G. William Domhoff in the first edition of *Who Rules America?* (1967). Over time, however, Mills's framework exerted considerable influence on the broader left. As Domhoff himself observed in 1968, the power-elite concept came to be seen as "the bridge between the Marxist and pluralist positions. . . . It is a necessary concept because not all national leaders are members of the upper class. In this sense, it is a modification and extension of the concept of a 'ruling class.'"[4]

The issue of whether a capitalist ruling class controls the state—or whether the state enjoys a degree of "relative autonomy"—was also central to the famous debate between Ralph Miliband, author of *The State in Capitalist Society* (1969), and Nicos Poulantzas, author of *Political Power and Social Classes* (1968). Their debate revolved around the extent of the state's independence from the capitalist class—an issue crucial to evaluating the possibilities for a social-democratic strategy for capturing state power.[5]

The debate reached a low point in the United States with Fred Block's influential 1977 essay, "The Ruling Class Does Not Rule." Block contended that the capitalist class lacked the class consciousness necessary to convert its economic dominance into political control. In this view, social democratic politics was entirely feasible within capitalism. After Biden defeated Trump in 2020, *Jacobin* republished Block's essay with a new epilogue in which he argued that—because the ruling class did not actually rule—Biden was free to pursue a New Deal–style, pro–working-class agenda that could prevent the return of a more capable and ruthless right-wing figure in 2024.

In light of the contradictions of the Biden administration and the return of Trump—with thirteen billionaires in his cabinet at the outset—the entire question of the ruling class and the state requires reexamination.

Neoliberalism and the U.S. Ruling Class

Although much of the Western left abandoned the concept of a ruling class in the late 1960s and 1970s, some thinkers resisted this shift. Sweezy consistently maintained in *Monthly Review* that the United States was governed by a capitalist ruling class. In *Monopoly Capital* (1966), Paul Baran and Sweezy argued that "a tiny oligarchy resting on vast economic power" controlled the nation's political and cultural institutions, making the notion of genuine U.S. democracy misleading at best.[6]

Except in times of crisis, the normal political system of

> capitalism, whether competitive or monopolistic, is bourgeois democracy. Votes are the nominal source of political power, and money is the real source: the system, in other words, is democratic in form and plutocratic in content. This is by now so well recognized that it hardly seems necessary to argue the case. Suffice it to say that all the political activities and functions which may be said to constitute the essential characteristics of the system—indoctrinating and propagandizing the voting public, organizing and maintaining political parties, running electoral campaigns—can be carried out only by means of money, lots of money. And since in monopoly capitalism the big corporations are the source of big money, they are also the main sources of political power.[7]

For Baran and Sweezy, ruling-class control over the state was evident in the constraints imposed on social spending, contrasted with the enormous military outlays and vast subsidies to business. Monopoly capitalism, they argued, was an "irrational system" plagued by overaccumulation: the wealthy and corporations held a quantity of money too large to profitably invest all of it in production. This leads to chronic economic stagnation as the "*normal* state" of monopoly capitalism.[8]

However, from the capitalist class's perspective, the 1970s crisis was blamed on the working class, accused of "squeezing" profits with demands for higher wages and allegedly causing a shortage of capital with which to invest—despite a lack of empirical support for this view.[9] In August 1971, only months before joining the U.S. Supreme Court, Lewis F. Powell, Jr., wrote his notorious memo to the U.S. Chamber of Commerce urging a coordinated neoliberal offensive against workers and the left, which were blamed for undermining "free enterprise." Ironically, just as parts of the left were abandoning the concept of a class-conscious U.S. ruling class, the U.S. oligarchy was reasserting its power and engineering a neoliberal restructuring across both major parties. In the 1980s, this took the institutional form of supply-side economics—Reaganomics—widely known as "Robin Hood in reverse."[10]

John Kenneth Galbraith had noted in *The Affluent Society* (1958) that the wealthy possessed a deep, longstanding fear of expropriation, treating even modest reforms that might limit their wealth as signs of impending revolution. The neoliberal era, marked by the reemergence of stagnation and intensified anxieties among the wealthy, brought a renewed assertion of ruling-class power aimed at dismantling the gains of the New Deal and the Great Society—gains wrongly blamed for capitalism's structural crisis.

The Neofascist Turn

The Great Financial Crisis/Great Recession (2007–2009) profoundly shook the U.S. financial oligarchy and the broader political system, accelerating major shifts in the structures of power. The rapid descent of the financial system toward a potential "nuclear meltdown" after the collapse of Lehman Brothers in September 2008 left both the capitalist class and the public in shock, with the crisis spreading globally.

The refusal of the Bush administration to bail out Lehman—motivated by conservative worries over "moral hazard"[11]—triggered cascading failures across the system. With the financial order on the brink, the Federal Reserve led an unprecedented rescue effort to protect capital, introducing "quantitative easing," effectively creating vast sums of money to stabilize financial markets. Trillions of dollars were funneled into the corporate sector to preserve the assets of the financial oligarchy.

The most alarming development for the U.S. capitalist class during the Great Financial Crisis was not simply the depth of the domestic recession; it was that, while the United States and the major economies of Europe and Japan plunged into severe contraction, China's economy barely paused before returning to near double-digit growth. From that moment, the decline of U.S.

economic hegemony—and the rise of a rival capable of challenging both the dollar and the global reach of U.S. monopoly-finance capital—became unmistakable.

Although the Great Recession helped elect Democrat Barack Obama, it also unleashed a radical-right insurgency centered in the lower-middle class—a movement that fiercely opposed mortgage relief, which it interpreted as aiding the upper-middle class above them and the working class below. Conservative talk radio had already attacked any form of government intervention. The spark came on February 19, 2009, when CNBC commentator Rick Santelli denounced Obama's housing plan as socialist, likened it to policies in Cuba, and complained that responsible homeowners were being forced to subsidize others' "bad decisions." Evoking the Boston Tea Party, Santelli inadvertently named the new movement. Within days, "Tea Party" organizations were forming across the country.[12]

The Tea Party quickly became libertarian-oriented and funded by major corporate interests—most famously the oil-and-chemical billionaire Koch brothers and their wider network of private equity–aligned donors. The Supreme Court's 2010 *Citizens United* decision removed most constraints on corporate and billionaire spending, opening the floodgates for dark money. That same year, eighty-seven Tea Party Republicans entered the House, along with Tea Party Senate candidates such as Marco Rubio. Their aim was not policy innovation but obstruction: to prevent the federal government from functioning. Their signature accomplishment was the 2011 Budget Control Act, which imposed spending caps and sequestration that choked off social expenditures, followed by the symbolic 2013 government shutdown. The Tea Party also helped mainstream the racist birther conspiracy theory that claimed Obama was a foreign-born Muslim.[13]

Despite its image as a grassroots upheaval, the Tea Party was essentially a creation of conservative media and billionaire patronage. Yet it revealed that conditions were ripe for sectors of monopoly-finance capital to mobilize large parts of the lower-middle class—overwhelmingly white, battered by neoliberalism, and steeped in nationalism, racism, patriarchy, and revanchism. This social stratum—lower-level managers, small proprietors, rural landowners, white evangelicals—occupies an intermediate class position: above the working class but below the professional-managerial class, and is anxious about downward mobility (fear of falling into the working class). It has characteristics of both the working class and the professional-managerial class and is ideologically inclined toward big capital.[14] This stratum was what Mills had referred to as "the rearguarders" of the system.[15] Historically, fascist movements emerge when the capitalist class feels threatened and liberal democracy proves incapable of managing deep economic and imperial contradictions; in such moments, capital turns to the lower-middle class and privileged layers of workers as its mass base. [16]

By 2013 the Tea Party's peak had passed, though it persisted in Washington through the House Freedom Caucus formed in 2015. By 2016, however, it was reborn as Donald Trump's Make America Great Again (MAGA) movement—a fully formed neofascist political bloc uniting sections of the U.S. ruling class with a mobilized lower-middle class. Trump selected Tea Party stalwart Mike Pence as his 2016 running mate, and in 2025 elevated Tea Party favorite Marco Rubio to Secretary of State. As Trump himself put it, "The Tea Party still exists—except now it's called Make America Great Again."[17]

Unlike the Tea Party, MAGA abandoned the outward appearance of fiscal conservatism—always a tool for dismantling liberal democracy rather than a real policy commitment. Yet it maintained a punitive, racist, and misogynistic ideology that appealed to its lower-middle-class base, and advanced a foreign policy that remained militaristic but recast U.S. dominance in ultranationalist terms. China became its defining enemy.

MAGA neofascism revived the "leader principle," treating the leader's actions as unchallengeable, while deepening the grip of the most reactionary sectors of the ruling class over the state. Classical fascism in Italy and Germany fused privatization with heightened state coercion and expanding militarism and imperialism.[18] Similarly, the crises produced by neoliberalism created the conditions for neofascism, yielding an uneasy but powerful alliance—"warring brothers"—between neoliberal and neofascist elites that now dominates the state and major media, anchored in the highest tiers of monopoly capital.[19]

The ruling class is not a single unified bloc. Its key factions—industrial, high-tech, energy, and financial—share an interest in maximizing wealth and minimizing regulation and taxes, but differ in their immediate concerns. Yet today, direct rule by a major fraction of the U.S. ruling class is unmistakable. As Thomas Piketty has shown in *Capital in the Twenty-First Century*, advanced capitalist countries remain grounded in family and dynastic wealth, despite new entrants to the billionaire class.[20] Claims that the system is run by a managerial elite or by a diffuse "corporate rich" have collapsed. The present reality is not conventional class struggle, but a class war prosecuted by capital and enforced through the state.[21]

Trump's backing came not from the traditional corporate giants but from privately held fortunes less constrained by regulation or public scrutiny. Trump himself, though a billionaire, is merely a vessel through which these forces pursue a political restructuring. As Scottish journalist and former MP George Kerevan observed, Trump is "a demagogue, but only a cipher for real class forces."[22]

The consolidation of a vast share of global funds in the hands of the U.S. monopoly-capitalist class has produced a financial oligarchy unprecedented in its wealth and dependence on state power. Nowhere is this more evident than in the high-tech sector, whose profits rely on military spending, defense-related technologies, stock-buybacks, and speculative stock buying by the wealthy. Trump's core capitalist support in 2024 came not from the Big Six tech monopolies (Apple, Amazon, Alphabet, Meta, Microsoft,

Nvidia) but from private tech wealth, private equity, and big oil. Prominent funders included:

- Tim Mellon (the grandson of Andrew Mellon, and heir to the Mellon banking fortune);
- Ike Perlmutter (former chair of Marvel Entertainment);
- Peter Thiel (cofounder of PayPal and owner of Palantir, a CIA-backed surveillance and data mining company—U.S. Vice President J. D. Vance is a Thiel protégé);
- Marc Andreessen and Ben Horowitz (two of the leading figures in Silicon Valley finance);
- Miriam Adelson (wife of the deceased casino billionaire Sheldon Adelson);
- Richard Uihlein (shipping magnate and heir of the Uihlein brewing—Schlitz beer—fortune); and
- Elon Musk (the world's richest man, owner of Tesla, X, and SpaceX, who provided over a quarter of a billion dollars to the Trump campaign).

Thanks to the unclear origin of dark money, the full list is unknowable, but it is clear that support by the tech oligarchs was central.[23]

The Biden administration had largely represented neoliberal capitalist interests making only limited, temporary concessions to workers. Biden had pledged to Wall Street before taking office that "nothing would fundamentally change." Yet in his January 2025 farewell address, he warned of an emerging oligarchy of "extreme wealth, power and influence" threatening democracy, rooted in concentrated ownership, "dark money," and the rise of a "tech-industrial complex." He even proposed 18-year term limits for Supreme Court justices—an acknowledgment, however belated, that the Court had become a stronghold of oligarchic rule.[24] No sitting U.S. president since Franklin D. Roosevelt has so sharply highlighted the issue of direct ruling-class control over the federal government—yet in Biden's case, this occurred only as he was leaving the White House.

These remarks, though unsurprising given longstanding elite dominance, reflected the new sense of a neofascist breakthrough. Kamala Harris had openly described Trump as a "fascist" during her campaign. In 2021 *Forbes* estimated the combined wealth of Biden's cabinet at $118 million.[25] Trump's 2025 cabinet and top appointees initially included thirteen billionaires with a total worth of $460 billion; their combined wealth dwarfed the $3.2 billion held by Trump's first-term cabinet.[26] (Of course, Musk—an early advisor in Trump's second term—had a net worth of about $400 billion.) In 2016 many leading capitalists were wary of Trump; by 2025, the government itself had become a billionaire's regime. According to Doug Henwood, this is less a sign of effective class rule than a symptom of its "rot."[27]

In Block's addendum to "The Ruling Class Does Not Rule," published by *Jacobin* in 2020, he argued that Biden had significant autonomy and could pursue pro–working-class reforms to prevent a worse authoritarian from emerging in 2024. But politicians in a capitalist society are not primarily accountable to voters. As the saying goes, "He who pays the piper calls the tune." Because their major donors barred any movement leftward, Democrats—represented in 2024 by Harris—lost millions of working-class voters who had supported Biden in 2020. Many did not turn to Trump; they simply exited electoral politics and joined what is effectively the country's largest political affiliation: the Party of Non-Voters.

What has emerged is not a repetition of Trump's earlier presidency but a far more open form of ruling-class governance, backed by a mobilized, revanchist lower-middle class, producing a right-wing neofascist state led by a president who has already breached constitutional boundaries and now presides over a near-imperial executive. Trump and Vance are closely tied to the Heritage Foundation and its Project 2025 blueprint. How far this political transformation will proceed—and whether it becomes institutionalized—depends on the ruling-class/MAGA alliance above and the struggle for popular hegemony below.

For decades, much of the Western left abandoned the concept of a ruling class, dismissing it as dogmatic or simplistic. In hindsight, this retreat reflected the intellectual habits of academia rather than the realities of political power during capitalism's structural crisis. *This severely hindered any real understanding of what sustained struggle requires in an era defined by capital's structural crisis.*

In 2022, Bernie Sanders countered this drift directly. In an article titled "The U.S. Has a Ruling Class and Americans Must Stand Up to It," he wrote:

> The most important economic and political issues facing this country are the extraordinary levels of income and wealth inequality, the rapidly growing concentration of ownership . . . and the evolution of this country into oligarchy. . . .
>
> We now have more income and wealth inequality than at any time in the last hundred years. In the year 2022, three multibillionaires own more wealth than the bottom half of American society—160 million Americans. Today, 45% of all new income goes to the top 1%, and CEOs of large corporations make a record-breaking 350 times what their workers earn. . . . In terms of political power, the situation is the same. A small number of billionaires and CEOs, through their Super Pacs, dark money and campaign contributions, play a huge role in determining who gets elected and who gets defeated. There are now an increasing number of campaigns in which Super Pacs actually spend more money on campaigns than the candidates, who become the puppets to their big money puppeteers. In the 2022 Democratic primaries, billionaires spent tens of millions trying to defeat progressive candidates who were standing up for working families.[28]

After the 2024 elections, Sanders noted that a Democratic Party that spent billions helping Israel wage "an all-out war against the entire Palestinian people" while neglecting domestic working-class needs saw its base abandon it—again, into the Party of Non-Voters. Some 150 billionaire families spent nearly $2 billion trying to shape the 2024 election, cementing a regime of open oligarchy. This has placed a plutocratic ruling class in power in the federal government that no longer even pretends to represent the interests of all. In resisting these tendencies, Sanders stated, "Despair is not an option. We are fighting not only for ourselves. We are fighting for our kids and future generations, and for the well-being of the planet."[29]

3

Monopoly Capital and the Structural Crisis of U.S. Capitalism

THE FIRST QUARTER-CENTURY AFTER the Second World War is often called the "golden age" of modern capitalism, marked by rapid economic growth and rising wages. This exceptional period rested on a unique convergence of historical conditions that proved highly favorable to expansion and prosperity. Among the most important were:

- the emergence of the United States as the hegemonic power in the capitalist world economy, reflected in the global dominance of the dollar, the expansion of the international trading system, and the creation of a dollar-based world oil market;
- the buildup of consumer savings (liquidity) during the Second World War, greatly expanding effective demand after the war;
- the rebuilding of the war-shattered economies of Western Europe and Japan;
- Cold War/imperialist military spending, including two major regional wars in Asia (in Korea and Vietnam);

- an era of cheap oil based in U.S. corporate domination of the Persian Gulf;
- a vast expansion of the "sales effort" to encourage people to consume more stuff;
- a new stage in the automobilization of the U.S. economy, including the construction of the interstate highway system, the reinforcement of the auto, steel, and glass industries, and the growth of suburbanization; and
- the rapid growth of foreign direct investment by multinational corporations centered in the advanced capitalist states.[1]

In *Monopoly Capital*, Paul A. Baran and Sweezy stressed that these conditions were historically specific and temporary. The unusually long postwar boom, they argued, would fade as these special supports weakened or disappeared. "The normal state of the monopoly capitalist economy is stagnation."[2]

Monopoly capitalism tends to generate slower economic growth than the more freely competitive capitalism of early industrialization. High profit margins based on monopoly pricing and intensified exploitation, combined with chronic excess productive capacity and persistent unemployment or underemployment, produce conditions of capital *overaccumulation*. More profits are generated than can be absorbed within the "real economy" through profit-making (productive) investment or capitalist consumption. Excess capacity, a structural feature of monopoly capitalism, discourages new investment in productive facilities, resulting in low net investment and sluggish growth. Although innovations continue to occur, they rarely have the economy-wide, transformative impact of earlier breakthroughs such as railroads, electricity, or automobiles. Many recent innovations, including much of the digital revolution, tend to be capital-saving rather than capital-absorbing and therefore do little to sustain long-term growth. The purpose of the wave of investments in data centers in the mid-2020s—stressing electric and water supplies—is to enhance artificial intelligence in order to save labor in the future.

Within a few years of *Monopoly Capital*'s publication, the decline of the postwar growth became visible. U.S. capacity utilization began a long-term downward trend. At the same time household liquidity gave way to rising consumer debt. The interstate highway system was largely completed. Western Europe and Japan, having rebuilt their economies, shifted to slower growth. At the same time, U.S. control over global oil prices weakened. Oil prices, long kept artificially low, rose in the early 1970s and then quadrupled following the OPEC embargo in response to U.S. support for Israel in the 1973 Arab-Israeli War. The resulting shock contributed to the deep recession of 1973–75 and ushered in a period of stagflation—inflation and stagnation occurring at the same time. Inflation, already rising in the 1960s, surged in the late 1970s, peaking at nearly 14 percent in 1981.

In effect, there was an erosion of the conditions that had underpinned the post–Second World War U.S. expansion, visible in:

- the initial decline of U.S. hegemony in the capitalist world economy, marked by Richard Nixon's ending of the convertibility of the dollar into gold in 1971;
- the end of liquidity in most consumer households with the shift from net savings to net indebtedness;
- renewed competition from the other industrial economies now rebuilt;
- the cessation of the Vietnam War—the second of the two regional wars in Asia that had powered U.S., and also German and Japanese, expansion;
- the end of cheap oil with the emergence of the Organization of the Petroleum Exporting Countries (OPEC) followed by the 1973 Arab-Israeli War;
- the saturation of consumer markets reducing the effectiveness of the "sales effort";

- the completion of the interstate highway system, and the end of the second wave of automobilization of the United States, including the major building of the suburbs;
- the beginnings of the movement of multinational corporations' factories abroad.[3]

With the waning of the historical factors that had produced the postwar boom, the economy tended to sink into its normal state of stagnation. This was partly compensated by the growth of financialization in the 1970s and '80s. The inflation rate was reduced by means of the Federal Reserve's sharp increases in interest rates, beginning with chairman Paul Volcker in the late 1970s, putting a damper on the economy by making it more expensive to borrow money. This led to a deep recession, resulting in an unemployment rate of over 10 percent. The subsequent gradual reduction in interest rates in order to stimulate the economy contributed to an *explosion of finance* that indirectly stimulated the economy but created a whole new debt structure imposed on top of the "real economy" of production of goods and services. The result was a structural crisis of capital reflected in a half-century of persistent economic stagnation, punctuated by financial bubbles, not only in the United States but in the rest of the advanced capitalist world as well.[4]

One way businesses have responded to slow growth is by introducing ever more new products as part of an increasingly costly sales effort. In the 1970s, roughly 1,000 new consumer products entered the market each year. By the mid-1980s, that figure had risen to about 5,000, and since the early 2000s it has reached 30,000 or more annually. Most of these "new products" are little more than variations on existing goods, designed to differentiate brands and encourage consumers—whose budgets are increasingly constrained—to increase their purchases, often by relying on credit.[5]

The slowdown in economic growth has been substantial, with the rate of GDP expansion falling from an average of 4.3 percent per year in the 1950s and '60s, to 3.2 percent in the '70s through the '90s, to 2.0 percent in the first two decades of the twenty-first century.[6] The economies of Britain, Germany, France, and Japan slowed even more over the same time span. Long periods of sluggish growth are endemic to monopoly capitalism, as argued by Baran and Sweezy in the 1960s—and by Harry Magdoff and Sweezy in the '70s, '80s, and '90s, in works such as *The End of Prosperity* (1977), *Stagnation and the Financial Explosion* (1986), and *The Irreversible Crisis* (1987). In this view, it is not the tendency to stagnation that requires explanation so much as exceptional periods of high growth rates, now few and far between.[7]

Growth has also slowed relative to population. Real (inflation-adjusted) *per capita GDP* growth fell from an annual average of 3.1 percent in the 1960s, to 2.2 percent in the 1970s and 1980s, 1.9 percent in the 1990s, 1.8 percent in the 2000s, and just 1.2 percent in the 2010s. By any measure, the "economic pie" is therefore expanding far more slowly than it once did. This slowdown has intensified pressure on businesses' relentless drive to accumulate ever larger amounts of capital.

A major response after the 2007–2009 Great Financial Crisis was an effort to stimulate the economy through a range of measures, including financial stimulus, bailouts of failing financial and nonfinancial firms, and the maintenance of near-zero interest rates for many years. Despite these interventions, job recovery after the crisis was the slowest since the Great Depression. The limited support for people harmed by the crisis, contrasted with the extensive rescue of corporations, has fueled much of the anger that persists today.

A significant stimulus to the economy over the past decades has been spending for climate-change related costs: from 2000 to 2025 this amounted to 7.7 trillion dollars. As the title of a Bloomberg article makes clear, "Disaster Recovery Is Big Business."[8] The AI investment boom directed at data centers, together with the consumption of the wealthy—with the top 10 percent responsible for nearly half of all consumption—kept the economy growing in 2025.

4

The Financialization of the Economy

"FINANCIALIZATION" IS A TERM USED to describe the huge increase in the relative role of finance in the U.S. economy, occurring in response to the slowing of GDP growth after the post–Second World War "golden age" decades. Financial companies make their profits on fees, interest on loans, and speculation. The outcome has been a new phase of monopoly-finance capital, increasingly dependent on low interest rates, rising debt levels, and periodic government bailouts.[1] As economic growth slowed following the post–Second World War era, nonfinancial corporations increasingly turned to finance as a primary way of employing their accumulating cash as well as to increase profits, with the aim of taking advantage of ever-increasing asset prices.

Financial profits are *not* made by producing a commodity and then selling it for a profit. Instead, money is made by utilizing it to make more money, without a tangible intermediate stage (M-M′ instead of M-C-M′, where M is money, C is a commodity or service, and M′ refers to more money than M). This occurs when a bank loans money to businesses to expand or to someone to purchase a car or a house. Nowadays there are non-bank lenders as well. Then there's speculation—with people "investing" in all sorts of imaginable bets, on stocks, on the future price of a commodity, on relative direction of two national currencies, future weather events, professional sports, etc. And new bets are created regularly. Goods industries also get into finance in a number of ways, such as creating a loan department to lend money to customers so they can purchase the product while the company makes money on the interest. Companies that do make commodities may also take on debt to speculate, hoping to drive up their stock prices. Finance, which had once been a small auxiliary component of the U.S. economy, has expanded so greatly that it is in a position of dominant economic importance.

Finance capital has turned a significant portion of the economy into a giant casino in which you can literally make bets on anything imaginable. This development is fed by the constant array of new financial "instruments." In addition, private equity (PE) firms get in on the act by buying established companies using leverage (debt taken out and put on the purchased company's books), and then sometimes selling off real estate or other parts. Using this scheme—buy it, strip it, flip it—enables financial capital to extract cash from its targets while leaving the purchased companies weakened, frequently filing for bankruptcy while workers lose their jobs (see sidebar for more details on PE and how it operates).

Although there was a long-running economic trend toward fewer companies in most sectors of production, private equity has encouraged even more consolidation in a number of industries. For example, the shortage of firefighting engines and ladder trucks made fighting the January 2025 fires in California that much more difficult. Slow production of new rigs and difficulty finding spare parts for older ones "have compounded in recent years as Wall Street executives led an aggressive consolidation of the industry in a plan to boost profit margins. One company, backed by a private equity firm, cut its own manufacturing lines as part of a streamlining strategy and then saw a backlog of fire engine orders soar

PRIVATE EQUITY (PE) AND THE ADVANTAGE OF LEVERAGE

"Thanks to modern tricks of financial engineering, investors can prosper even when the underlying business is failing."[2]

PE firms are a type of financial company. They raise money to invest in companies that are not publicly traded (listed on the stock market). The original justification for PE deals is that they would purchase companies in trouble, turn them around by their magical management abilities, and then sell the now healthy company. PE firms solicit large investments from rich people (minimums of $250,000 to millions of dollars) who then become "limited partners." Despite the myth of how they function, funds raised by the "vulture capitalist" PE firms are routinely used to purchase a company, which is then commonly loaded up with debt by taking out a loan in the name of the purchased company, amassing enormous returns. This is known as a "leveraged buyout." The rate of return on funds invested skyrockets when debt (leverage) is used to increase returns on investments/speculation.

In addition, parts of the purchased companies such as the land they are on or the buildings they use—are sold, forcing them to pay off debt and/or pay for expenses such as rent, that they never had to pay before. Purchased companies, frequently not able to manage the loan payments, are then cannibalized by firing many workers and selling any real estate and other assets.

The share of profits that goes to fund managers when they sell investments is referred to as "carried interest." The income of PE firms that goes to fund managers is taxed at a low rate, as if it were capital gains, rather than as ordinary income, with the general partners gaining significant savings on their tax bill. This process has been described by an Oxford University professor as constituting a "billionaire factory."[3]

into billions of dollars." General president of the International Association of Fire Fighters, Edward Kelly, said that while the pandemic may have brought on problems, *"it was masking what ends up being a main driver of higher cost and lag time in production: the monopolizing of fire truck and ambulance manufacturing in the United States. . . . At the end of the day, absent competition, monopoly capitalism is a shakedown."*[4] So, at the same time that fires are more prevalent and destructive, it becomes harder to obtain the proper resources needed to fight fires.

Despite a business model that involves pillaging and destroying companies while workers lose their jobs, private equity firms receive special tax treatment on their profits. This has occurred in healthcare with buying up what were smaller, nonprofit and community hospitals, selling off the land, reducing staff numbers, and then charging rent to the "new" hospital, which cannot afford to pay. This is not only incredible *chutzpah*, but also criminal in its effects on workers and public health. With staff reductions and other cost-saving schemes, patients are more likely to have adverse outcomes, including death, in for-profit hospitals. In 2024 a number of state legislatures considered restricting PE's destructive activities in the healthcare sector.[5]

Hedge funds use a more short-term type of speculation than private equity and provide an "alternate" type of investment (or speculation) than other assets. Hedge fund managers were supposedly earning approximately 2 percent of the assets they managed plus 20 percent of any profits, providing for huge returns. But apparently, using clever maneuvering, hedge fund managers actually reap about half of all profits.[6]

The "private capital" sector, consisting of non-publicly traded private companies, often loans funds to businesses instead of purchasing them. Here funds are raised from wealthy individuals, insurance companies, pension funds, and so on. These companies then provide predatory loans to businesses that are finding it difficult to borrow from banks.

Financialization has penetrated most sectors of the economy and is inextricably linked to the general monopolization trend. Government policy and actions/inactions have actively promoted economic consolidation.[7] To promote mergers and acquisitions, the federal government, as a way of feeding the financialization process, removed a whole set of restrictions dating back to the New Deal era, notably separating commercial from investment banking. This has led to vast new waves of finance-induced corporate concentration. Fewer firms controlling a large share of the market means that monopolies/oligopolies have greater power to raise prices and generate higher profit margins (markups over prime production costs), as well as greater power to restrain wages. By the time of the Great Financial Crisis in 2008, the top two hundred corporations alone accounted for around 30 percent of gross profits in the U.S. economy—an economy that included 5.5 million corporations, 2 million partnerships, 17.7 million non-farm sole proprietorships, and 1.8 million farm sole proprietorships.[8]

"Deindustrialization" had little to do directly with foreign competition, but rather with a number of other factors such as: (1) corporations moving factories to the southern United States and outside U.S. territorial limits to try to avoid workers unionizing and to escape environmental regulations; (2) the search for lower unit labor costs through shifts to regions and countries where the gains from low wages outweighed any losses in relative productivity (a process known as the global labor arbitrage)—a shift made possible by revolutions in communications and transportation; (3) the decision of private corporations not to modernize their factories (as in the case of steel), preferring financial investments instead; and (4) the general shift from production to finance within the economy. In the late 1960s and 1970s there was a wave of mergers with, or acquisition of, other companies. As corporations bought up or merged with other companies they tended to shed aspects of the businesses, which while profitable, were not making satisfactory profits. Many plants were closed in the process and the workers let go.[9]

As the global business correspondent for Bloomberg Opinion describes the ever-increasing corporate concentration:

> The consolidation of capitalism is most advanced in the US, the leading economic power, and in tech and finance, the cutting edge of the new economy, suggesting that oligopoly is the way of the future. Five tech companies are each worth more than $1 trillion, and one, Apple Inc., is worth more than $3 trillion. Three big investment houses, BlackRock Inc., the Vanguard Group Inc., and State Street Corp., collectively manage around $22 trillion in assets. Over the past two decades, three out of four US industries have grown more concentrated.[10]

Economic crises under capitalism, it bears repeating, are almost invariably attributed by capital to high wages and too generous working conditions, low labor-productivity increases, and government interference. Although seldom in accord with the truth, such claims have the advantage that they justify a policy of taking from workers and the poor and giving to the rich. Even though the tendency to economic stagnation was fairly apparent, orthodox economics, reflecting its primarily ideological function, generally ignored or kept quiet about the issue before the extremely sluggish recovery from the Great Financial Crisis/Great Recession of 2007–2009. Even now the full depth of the secular stagnation problem is mostly downplayed.

It has been repeatedly shown that, under conditions of monopoly-finance capital, a rising surplus of funds flowing to corporations and the wealthy primarily fuels higher asset prices and the concentration of wealth at the top of society rather than productive investment outside of the financial sector. Although the share of net investment in GDP—that is, investment in the real economy—has stagnated over the long term, and corporations are holding trillions of dollars in idle cash, capital continues to advance the same claim: there is a shortage of capital and the wealthy lack sufficient resources to generate new investment.

That narrative is used to justify repeated demands for public assistance to business, such as tax abatements, publicly funded infrastructure to support private projects, and policies of economic austerity.[11] It also underpins calls for lower taxes on corporations and the wealthy, cast as indispensable "job creators." The pursuit of these strategies has systematically increased capital's power relative to labor, the state, and the global economy. This broader restructuring of the political economy, including efforts to subordinate the state more fully to the logic of capital, is commonly described as neoliberal globalization.[12]

Neoliberalism was a response to slowing economic growth and profits that were considered insufficient by business. But in the neoliberal era, the economy has grown ever more slowly despite the fact that financialization and speculation have served to lift it for brief periods through what came to be known as the *wealth effect*. This refers to the stimulation of greater luxury consumption by the wealthy as their financial assets increase—buying private planes, yachts, and even larger mansions, etc. This helps to boost the economy for short periods of time, even when investment is stagnant.

Today, financialization is fully embedded in the economy and has extended to the manipulation of personal financial flows beyond regular income. This occurs through methods that are more systematic and predatory than in the past, including the raiding of private and public pensions, the extraction of revenue from government-financed health insurance programs, the imposition of much higher interest rates on the poor, and the inflation of pharmaceutical prices.

Manufacturing output increased substantially up to the Great Recession and has changed little since. In contrast, the expansion of finance relative to manufacturing has been dramatic. During the 1970s and 1980s, financial profits were less than half of manufacturing profits; since 2000, they have averaged about 50 percent higher than those of manufacturing.[13]

At the height of Wall Street bubbles, large parts of the population are drawn in. Before the housing bubble burst in the Great Recession/Great Financial Crisis of 2007–2009, low interest rates allowed homeowners to refinance and take out second mortgages based on an increase in home values so that their spending could go up even if wage incomes did not. However, the increased levels of household debt pushed many into bankruptcy when the crisis came.

As we write in 2026, a new explosion of debt and speculation is being encouraged by Trump's policies. Andrew Ross Sorkin, author of *1929: Inside the Greatest Crash in Wall Street History—and How It Shattered a Nation*, has described how

> we are in the grip of a sweeping new age of financialization and innovation—the boldest transformation in money and investing since the 1920s—that is also driven by the idea of expanding access to markets. Private equity, venture capital and private credit, once the preserve of institutions and wealthy individuals, are now about to be repackaged for the masses, even woven into 401(k) retirement plans. Crypto tokens are being sold as a way to buy slices of private firms like SpaceX and OpenAI, in the gray zone of securities law.
>
> It all comes amid a new stock boom, fueled by a mania for A.I., and with a new administration in Washington that is determined to loosen rules—creating a permissive spirit similar to the one that passed for innovation in the 1920s. The Trump administration is working on rolling back key provisions of the Dodd-Frank Act, easing capital requirements for midsize banks and sidelining the Consumer Financial Protection Bureau—an agency born after 2008 to police predatory lending. Congress, for its part, has advanced measures like the Genius Act and, more recently, the so-called Financial Innovation and Technology for the 21st Century Act—billed

as modernization and, in practice, opening the gates for crypto and other speculative products.[14]

What could possibly go wrong?

Finance vs. Workers

The growth of finance in the economy has harmed working people in a number of ways. These include:

a) **Job losses.** Mergers and acquisitions aimed at increasing economic concentration often lead to restructuring at labor's expense. Job losses are also common when private equity firms acquire companies, strip them of value, and sell them if anything remains—in effect, "buy it, strip it, flip it."
b) **Greater corporate concentration.** Financialization accelerates the consolidation of business, leaving fewer firms in each sector with greater power to charge oligopolistic or monopolistic prices and control wages.
c) **Misallocation of economic surplus.** Surplus that could have been used to meet people's needs is instead funneled into stock buybacks, financial divisions, and speculative activities.
d) **Expropriation of workers' income and assets.** Financial firms extract income from workers in multiple ways, including through pension funds drawn into speculative investments controlled by private companies that are not publicly traded and are not required to disclose detailed financial information. The lack of transparency surrounding such firms creates serious risks for workers. As a result, "unions negotiating for employee rights and protections may lack critical financial information about companies employing tens of thousands of workers."[15]
e) **Expansion of household debt.** People are aggressively encouraged to take on future obligations, such as household and credit card debt. Young people who cannot obtain credit cards, and those who have exhausted other borrowing

options, are often steered toward buy-now-pay-later (BNPL) loans, which carry high interest rates and deepen indebtedness. Black communities are especially harmed, facing higher costs associated with disinvested neighborhoods and ongoing discrimination in housing markets. Black home-buyers, for example, are about twice as likely to be denied a mortgage as white buyers with the same income.[16]

f) **Exposure to financial bubbles.** As finance-driven bubbles grow, many people feel pressure to participate, sometimes by using retirement savings. When these bubbles inevitably burst, households can lose homes, savings, or both.

Debt Stimulates the Economy

Although the expansion of debt with financialization can cause significant problems when people take on too much debt or bubbles burst, it does help to keep the economy growing. When individuals or businesses take out loans to make purchases, they stimulate the economy by spending money they otherwise would not have had. Similarly, when governments spend more than they collect in taxes and run deficits, the accumulation of public debt can also boost economic activity.

Since the 1970s, the expansion of debt relative to the size of the economy has been dramatic. Private (non-government) debt surged from less than 100 percent of GDP in the 1970s to more than 250 percent by the end of 2007, creating a highly precarious and unstable situation. When the bubble burst in 2007, leading to the bankruptcy of Lehman Brothers, the fourth-largest investment bank in the United States, in September 2008, what is known as the Great Financial Crisis/Great Recession deepened and many people were hurt financially.

The deleveraging of private debt (households and business) during and following the Crisis of 2007–2009—as people and businesses went bankrupt or lost property when unable to pay back loans—was dramatic and contributed to the very slow recovery that followed. The total number of workers employed didn't reach pre-recession levels until May 2014, about six and a half years after the start of the recession.

Following the Great Recession, which officially ended in June 2009, debt decreased (deleveraging) in the private sector especially in household and financial business. However, in stepped government debt as money was poured into the economy to save companies and to help maintain the population. There was another large jump in government debt in response to the COVID-19 pandemic, helping companies and the public, and even temporarily reducing U.S. poverty rates.

The Significance of Government Spending and Debt

The federal government can continue spending even when tax revenues are insufficient by issuing Treasury bonds and notes through the financial system. Since the post–Second World War era, government spending has been a key factor in stabilizing the economy. This role becomes especially important when spending is deficit-financed—that is, when the government spends money that it does not collect from taxes on individuals or corporations.

Since the 1950s there have been just a handful of years when the federal government *did not* spend more than it took in. The lion's share (today about 70 percent) of federal government expenditure on goods and services is devoted to the military, while federal government borrowing (and hence its interest payments) is heavily military-induced. Gargantuan amounts are spent on the Pentagon, running, at the end of the Biden administration, at almost $800 billion a year in terms of *acknowledged* military spending (in reality reaching $1.5 trillion a year when *unacknowledged* military spending hidden elsewhere in the government budget is included).[17]

On the basis of acknowledged U.S. military expenditures alone, the United States spends more on war and war preparations than the combined spending of the next nine countries—China, Russia, India, Saudi Arabia, Germany, France, South Korea, Japan, and Ukraine. [18] Military spending serves the double purpose of supporting individual corporations and providing effective demand for the economy—even more so when it is based on debt— while also expanding the U.S. empire and serving to promote the interests of monopoly capital throughout the globe. However, the increase of military spending is limited, given the preponderance of U.S. military power already deployed around the world—and large wars inevitably lead to catastrophic destruction. The United States is behind the continuing NATO proxy war with Russia in Ukraine, which had its origins in the eastward expansion of NATO. Washington has also been supplying weapons for Israel in its genocide aimed at the Palestinian people. On February 28, 2026, the United States and Israel jointly launched a major war on Iran and invasion of Lebanon, the full ramifications of which are not yet apparent. In 2017, the first Trump administration commenced a new Cold War on China and today it is preparing for a limited nuclear war with Beijing over Taiwan (internationally recognized as part of China, though under a separate governance). Yet, despite U.S. military interventions around the world in recent decades (Afghanistan, Iraq, Iran, Libya, Nigeria, Somalia, Syria, Venezuela, Yugoslavia) and the new Cold War on China, national defense spending, set to increase by 50 percent in 2027, has as yet been insufficient stimulus to lift the economy out of stagnation.[19]

While private debt was decreasing (being "deleveraged") in the aftermath of the Great Financial Crisis/Great Recession, U.S. government debt expanded so much that the federal debt in 2024 was near 100 percent of the GDP, a level not seen since the Second World War. A period of rapid debt increase occurred in the 1980s through early 1990s. The second was during the 2007–2009 Great Financial Crisis and its aftermath, through around 2014. The third huge increase was in response to the COVID-19 pandemic, especially in 2020. Civilian government spending on consumption and investment (goods and services) as a percentage of GDP has remained fairly stable throughout the post–Second World War period, but military spending, transfer payments, and net interest are all now increasing relative to GDP. The vast quantities of federal funds created by monetary easing (essentially printing money), which served to bail out corporations to the tune of trillions of dollars, brought the economy out of the 2007–2009 crisis and then again from the brief recession caused by the disruption of the COVID-19 pandemic. Yet, although corporate wealth soared as a result, the majority of the population ended up relatively worse off, while at the same time responsible for more and more public debt. As Karl Marx wrote, "The only part of the national wealth that actually enters into the collective possession of a modern nation is—the national debt."[20]

Crypto Currencies

This financial innovation began around 2009 with the creation of private digital payment systems. Ownership records are maintained electronically on decentralized blockchain networks, allowing users to make transactions without relying on government-backed currencies or banks. Cryptocurrencies have been particularly useful for illegal transactions and tax avoidance.

Bitcoin, the largest cryptocurrency by market value, was designed to allow "mining," a process that uses massive amounts of energy to solve mathematical problems. The number of new Bitcoins is programmed to slow gradually and the creation of new coins will eventually stop, making the total supply finite. Many other cryptocurrencies, however, have no limit on how many can be issued. Other types of crypto include *stablecoins*, which are pegged to the dollar or another currency, and *meme coins*, which are based on internet memes and have no intrinsic value.

Cryptocurrencies have become major instruments of speculation and market influence, often to the detriment of working people. Mining consumes enormous amounts of energy, imposing significant environmental costs. Additionally, crypto ventures like the Trump family's World Liberty Financial illustrate how such systems can be used legally by the wealthy to gain both access and influence.

Harry Magdoff and Paul Sweezy, writing some forty to fifty years ago in *Monthly Review* articles and books,[21] identified the financialization of the U.S. economy as a response to persistent stagnation of the "real" economy of goods and services. As finance has evolved to become an ever more dominant part of the economy and, as its associated problems have intensified, even some conservatives have grown concerned about the phenomenon. Oren Cass, an economist who founded American Compass and served on the advisory board of Project 2025, exemplifies this shift. His think tank describes itself as "charting the course for conservative economics." In an opinion piece for the *New York Times*, Cass wrote:

> In a financialized economy, businesses become mere sources of cash, assets to be manipulated and then operated for maximum investor returns. Workers become just another cost, like lumber. Customers are just revenue streams to be tapped. . . . It contributes to the breakdown in solidarity among citizens, with disastrous ramifications in the political arena, and weakens national security, with serious consequences abroad. It promotes reckless practices within financial markets that even in recent memory plunged the economy into deep recession. The capitalists driving financialization and promoting its results have become capitalism's worst enemy. Every consumer and every worker in the United States feels the effects.[22]

5

Capital Fights for an Even Larger Slice of the Pie

THE WEALTHY ARGUE THAT WORKERS don't need a larger share of the economic pie. Instead, they claim that if the size of the overall pie grows, everyone will benefit—a notion often summed up as "a rising tide lifts all boats." In other words, they suggest that as the rich get richer, some of that wealth will trickle down to workers and the poor.

In practice, however, capitalists have consistently fought to secure an ever-larger share for themselves, especially during periods of slow or stagnant growth. There are several ways businesses and the wealthy increase and protect their wealth, some outside the normal course of accumulation. Companies can consolidate by outcompeting or buying up rivals, gaining greater market share and increased market power. They also seek tax reductions or incentives from local, state, and federal governments—a common practice that significantly boosts profits.[1]

Another key method is squeezing labor: as workers use machines to transform raw materials into finished products, a growing portion of the value added above prime production costs goes to capital rather than labor. For these strategies to succeed, the balance of power must heavily favor capital.

Ultimately, businesses and the wealthy aim to maximize profits and private riches. They recognize that the most effective way to achieve this is by minimizing taxes, avoiding regulations—whether labor, environmental, or financial—and limiting labor's ability to negotiate higher pay or better working conditions.

Power—particularly concentrated economic and political power—is seldom addressed in mainstream economic and political discussions. Yet the distribution of power across society shapes which laws and regulations are enacted, how they are enforced, and the overall conditions faced by workers.

During the Great Depression of the 1930s, several pro-labor laws were enacted. The National Labor Relations Act (1935) guaranteed workers the right to form unions. The Fair Labor Standards Act (1938) established a minimum wage, a 40-hour workweek, and mandatory overtime pay. These legal protections, combined with widespread organizing efforts, led to a substantial increase in union membership. As a result, labor became a powerful force capable of challenging capital and securing significant improvements in working conditions and living standards.

The rapid growth of the labor movement in the 1930s and 1940s led to union membership peaking at about one-third percent of workers during the 1950s and 1960s. In these decades, real wages—adjusted for inflation—rose alongside productivity, enabling many workers to enjoy a more comfortable standard of living. Employer-funded retirement pensions also became common. The steady increase in workers' real wages helped expand the economy by boosting effective demand, which in turn encouraged capital investment. However, businesses viewed this as a mixed blessing: although after-taxes corporate profit margins often reached double digits during business cycle peaks in the 1940s and 1950s, they were constrained by high taxes and rising wages as well as other forms of worker compensation.[2]

From the 1970s onward, as the "golden age" elapsed and economic stagnation deepened, capital increasingly focused on protecting and expanding profit margins by extracting more value from workers. This occurred both in workers' roles as producers and as consumers, with a growing share of the total economic output concentrated in the hands of a tiny group of centi-millionaires and billionaires.

Class Warfare

In capitalist societies, there is a constant struggle between workers and employers. Businesses aim to secure the cheapest labor possible and maintain working conditions that favor profits, while workers seek higher wages and better conditions. This conflict was evident even during the New Deal era of the 1930s. Although national labor protections were being enacted, businesses actively undermined union organizing by placing spies within unions. According to U.S. Senate committee hearings, companies paid for "a unique service—Union-Prevention and Union-Smashing. Industrialists who bought the service wanted to know about their workers' attempts to organize. They paid $80,000,000 a year to keep their plants from becoming unionized, or if they were unionized, to break up the union. There is no longer any doubt about it. The record is clear."[3]

While periods of favorable conditions sometimes allow labor to make significant gains, businesses consistently work to reverse those gains or block new ones. As labor historian David Montgomery noted, "No historical resolution of the conflict between wage labor and capital has enjoyed a permanent lease on life."[4]

In response to the shift in power toward labor during the New Deal and the Second World War, capital pushed back through legislation and broad anti-labor measures. The Taft-Hartley Act of 1947 was the first major step, followed by a series of policies during the McCarthy/Red Scare era of the late 1940s through the 1950s.

The initial targets were the communist- and socialist-led unions in the Congress of Industrial Organizations (CIO). Conservative union leaders, seeking closer alignment with business interests, joined the effort to suppress radical unionism. Ten radical unions were expelled from the CIO, and militant union practices were systematically attacked, particularly those aimed at organizing and striking. These efforts also limited unions' involvement in broader political and economic issues, restricting them largely to immediate "bread and butter" concerns of their members.[5]

The wealthy and corporate elite tend to blame economic crises on workers, government intervention, and external forces—never on the capitalist system itself. Whether crises are real or perceived, they create openings for major policy shifts. The solution proposed by the wealthy is consistently the same: transfer income and wealth from workers to capital owners.

When economic troubles and stagnation emerged in the 1970s, capitalists deployed multiple strategies to increase their power over workers and society. A crucial early move in this campaign was Powell's 1971 memo to the U.S. Chamber of Commerce,[6] discussed above, in the document, titled "ATTACK ON AMERICAN FREE ENTERPRISE SYSTEM," he laid out the forces he imagined were destroying the ability of capital to do as it pleases. The list is long and includes the usual suspects such as labor unions, radical organizations, colleges, and the media. As strange as it might seem, Powell selected consumer safety advocate Ralph Nader as "perhaps the single most effective antagonist of American business." Likewise the best seller *The Greening of America* by Charles Reich, according to Powell, was "a frontal assault . . . on our government, our system of justice, and the free enterprise system." Powell maintained that it all added up to a "broad, shotgun attack on the system itself . . . which undermine[s] confidence and confuse[s] the public." For example, he wrote, with respect to "proposals for tax incentives through changes in depreciation rates and investment credits, that "these are usually described in the media as 'tax breaks,' 'loopholes,' or 'tax benefits' for the *benefit of business*." Isn't that just shocking? How else should they be described?

Powell's memo aimed to galvanize the Chamber of Commerce and the broader business community, providing a road map for fighting back against "anti-business" forces. Twenty-six years later, in 1997, the Chamber's *Nation's Business* magazine reported that it had "developed and successfully implemented a strategy based on the [Powell] memorandum." The result? "The Chamber has helped create a political climate in which the debate in Congress and between Congress and the White House is no longer on how much more to tax, spend, and regulate but on how much less to tax, spend, and regulate." Notably, the spending cuts never targeted corporate subsidies or military budgets—only programs serving workers and the poor. The incoming Chamber CEO planned to confront "labor-union leaders who would savage good companies," trial lawyers who had "manipulated and abused" the judicial system, and "extreme environmentalists who have thrown common sense and sound science out the window."[7]

The Powell memo and Chamber response were part of a larger movement. Other conservative figures wrote influential books during this period, including William Simon, U.S. Treasury secretary from 1974 to 1977. His books *A Time for Truth* (1978) and *A Time for Action* (1980) expressed alarm about what was "happening to my country," leaving him "frightened and angry."[8] Conservative think tanks and foundations either launched or expanded their activities during this era.[9]

During capitalism's "golden age" corporations faced challenges in increasing their profit margins, given resistance from their workforces, impacting their desired bottom lines. In 1969, the *Wall Street Journal* reported that "many manufacturing executives openly complained in recent years . . . [that] too much control had passed from management to labor."[10] A 1974 *Business Week* special issue on the debt economy argued that in an era of slow growth, a strong economy required strong corporations. The solution, according to the magazine, was to shift resources and wealth from workers to big business in response to low profitability:

> It is inevitable that the U.S. economy will grow more slowly than it has. . . . Some people will obviously have to do with less . . . Indeed, cities and states, the home mortgage market, small business, and the consumer, will all get less than they want because the basic health of the U.S. is based on the basic health of its corporations and banks: the biggest borrowers and the biggest lenders. . . .
>
> Put simplistically, as long as corporations stay healthy, they can pay taxes and provide people with jobs. . . . But when corporations fall sick, people lose jobs and stop buying. Nobody pays taxes, governments and local authorities are not financed, and everyone—corporations, consumers, federal and local administrations alike—goes broke or gets embedded more deeply in the debt spiral . . .
>
> *Yet it will be a hard pill for many Americans to swallow—the idea of doing with less so that big business can have more.* It will be particularly hard to swallow because it is quite obvious that if big business and big banks are the most visible victims of what ails the Debt Economy, they are also in large measure the cause of it . . .
>
> Nothing that this nation, or any other nation, has done in modern history compares in difficulty with the selling job that must now be done to make people accept the new reality. And there are grave doubts whether the job can be done at all. Historian Arnold Toynbee, filled with years and compassion, laments that democracy will be unable to cope with approaching economic problems—and that totalitarianism will take its place.[11]

Similarly, Simon thought that the needed remedy might be hard for many to take: "I believe the situation can be changed—The sickness can be cured. The medicine won't be pleasant."[12]

However, the "selling job" and the "hard pill" of the "medicine" proved relatively easy to impose on the country because they were marketed as eventually benefiting everyone. The pitch was simple: the public would get cheaper products and there would be more jobs, which would offset any temporary "dislocations" caused by policies designed to boost corporate profits. However, the actual consequences have been severe. Workers have been squeezed hard by "free trade" agreements and the war on unions.

There are six primary ways to increase profits:

1) Suppress wages.
2) Increase worker productivity.
3) Sell more existing products.
4) Develop new products and convince people to buy them.
5) Eliminate environmental, safety, and financial regulations that reduce profit margins.
6) Relocate production to regions with lower unit labor costs.

Neoliberalism pursued all these profit-enhancement strategies while also cutting taxes and expanding the financial sector. This required capital to gain greater control over the government, which was justified by calls for deregulation and reduced government involvement in the economy and society.

Union membership began declining in the mid-1960s as jobs shifted from manufacturing to services, but the drop accelerated sharply in the 1980s. The turning point came when Ronald Reagan fired striking air traffic controllers and replaced them temporarily with military controllers acting as strikebreakers. This made anti-union propaganda and action more socially "acceptable" among businesses, government, and mass media. As Harry Magdoff observed in 1983: "The significance of the Reagan administration is that it is open, outright, a class-biased system. No bones about it. It's for the rich, has a theoretical system to justify it, and it is against the poor. And then it violates its own principles at every point where it's necessary to protect the rich. I think it's as simple as that."[13]

Capital's assault on labor, combined with growth in the largely non-unionized service sector, caused union membership to plummet from roughly one-third of workers to about 10 percent today (now including roughly one-third of government workers but less than 6 percent of private-sector workers). This decline in union strength is reflected in fewer strikes. The 1970s was the last decade with significant strike activity, averaging nearly 300 work stoppages involving 1,000 or more workers and 26 million lost workdays annually (Figure 5.1).[14]

Strike numbers collapsed in the 1980s and have averaged only 15 significant strkes per year since 2010. As union membership fell, so did the wage premium for union workers. In construction, for example, union membership dropped from 40 percent in the 1970s to 10 percent in the early 2020s. During the same period, union construction workers' pay advantage shrank from 70 percent above the average U.S. worker to about 15 percent above average.[15]

High rates of union membership benefit workers far beyond union members themselves. When unions negotiate better contracts, wages for nonunion workers in similar jobs often rise as well. Similarly, when the minimum wage increases, workers earning slightly above the new floor typically receive raises too.

The assault on unions intensified with the rise of the financialized economy in the 1980s. Financialization depends on extracting ever-larger streams from the income/assets of workers in the "real economy" of goods and services production. This drove capital—and the government it influences—to adopt more aggressive tactics aimed at weakening labor.

Union activity increased beginning in 2022, with workers organizing at previously non-union companies and striking in greater numbers than in years. The 2023 United Auto Workers strike victory was particularly impressive, helping pave the way for workers at a Volkswagen plant in Tennessee to vote overwhelmingly to

Figure 5.1: Annual Work Stoppages of 1,000 or More Workers (10-yr. moving average)

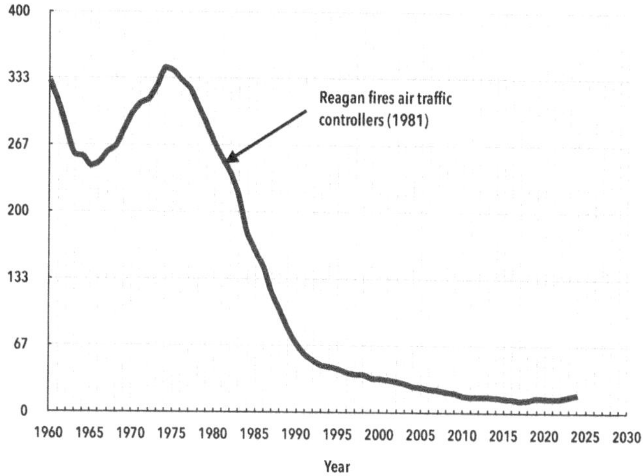

Sources and Notes: Bureau of Labor Statistics (BLS), "Annual work stoppages involving 1,000 or more workers, 1947 - Present."

unionize in April 2024. Apple store workers in Maryland won their first contract in 2024. Unions have formed among graduate students, Starbucks employees, and even Disneyland character performers. However inspiring these victories are, labor organizing and contract battles remain nowhere near the levels seen from the postwar 1940s through the 1970s. Companies aggressively fight each union drive and delay contract negotiations after unions form.

Capital's war on unions has only accelerated this century. Companies like Amazon, Starbucks, and Trader Joe's have "[mounted] a fierce counterattack against union drives," deploying new surveillance tools to fight workers.[16] A 2023 Economic Policy Institute fact sheet reports "Employers Are Charged with Violating Federal Law in Nearly 40% of Union Elections."[17] Corporations including Amazon, SpaceX, and Trader Joe's are even attempting to dismantle the New Deal-era National Labor Relations Act, a crucial worker protection. Amazon claims the National Labor Relations Board itself—the agency tasked with protecting the right to unionize—is unconstitutional.[18] Because of economic uncertainty, workers are less likely to quit jobs than they once were, further strengthening employers' hand. As a January 2025 *Wall Street Journal* headline declared: "Balance of Power Shifts Back Toward Bosses."[19] Of course, the balance was never truly in labor's favor—workers simply had a brief period of slightly improved bargaining leverage.

The mass firing of federal workers in early 2025 during Trump's second term left them without severance pay, unable to pay bills, and without health insurance. The administration terminated contracts with government unions covering over twenty agencies—including the Environmental Protection Agency, Veterans Administration, and Department of Agriculture—affecting one million workers. Private companies take their cues from the federal government's treatment of labor, as demonstrated by the more aggressive tactics businesses adopted after Reagan fired air traffic controllers in the early 1980s. Companies will now find it more acceptable to treat workers harshly.

Union membership and militancy grew in the 1930s and 1940s, and by the decades following the Second World War about one-third of workers belonged to unions. It's no coincidence that during this same period, the income share of the top 1 percent fell from 25–30 percent to just about 10 percent by the 1970s. But as union strength declined—accelerating in the 1980s—the top 1 percent's income share climbed back to about 25 percent.[20] Union density in the mid-2020s has returned to the low levels not seen since the early twentieth century, before the great wave of union growth began.

Following the 2007–2009 Great Financial Crisis, it became increasingly clear that monopoly-finance capitalism demanded ever-greater extraction of wealth from the broader population. All forms of support—including wages, pensions, health insurance, public education funding, and welfare—came under attack. These neoliberal responses to capitalism's structural crisis have increased the power, income, and wealth of capital at the expense of working and lower-middle classes, with devastating effects on labor.

The wealthy pursued other means of concentrating wealth with equal vigor, pushing "reforms" that weakened enforcement of labor and environmental regulations while cutting taxes on corporate profits and high incomes.[21]

When proposals backed by large majorities call for raising taxes on the wealthy and corporations, capitalists today cry "class war." Yet when questioned about their own class war on labor, representatives of the capitalist class typically claim class does not exist. In a rare moment of candor, billionaire investor Warren Buffett explained when asked whether class war existed: "There's class warfare, all right, but it's my class, the rich class, that's making war, and we're winning."[22] The current phase of class war—underway for more than half a century—is the one waged by capital against labor. As journalist Hamilton Nolan explained in 2023:

> Class war. It is the war we are all living through, in the land of the free. Look at all of politics through this lens, and everything snaps into focus, like the eye doctor finally presenting you with the right prescription. . . . "Politics," for the most part, is directly downstream from class war. Electoral politics is nothing but one more good investment for the investor class. Fund politicians for millions of dollars, and reap billions of dollars in benefits via tax cuts and deregulation on the back end. Religious zealots and other varieties of true believers are enlisted as front line troops in economic battles that masquerade as culture wars. Regular working people are made to fight about racism and yell at poor immigrants and channel their very real dissatisfaction at their thwarted dreams into anger about Bud Light and Target and who can go into which restroom. And the investor class harvests their votes and chuckles and p3sses the tax cut and couldn't

really give a damn about the outcome of all the rest of it. This is "politics" in America in a nutshell.[22]

As Michael Sainato reported in *The Guardian* in 2023:

> Intense pushback against unionization is becoming the norm in the US—and it is having an impact. The intense opposition from many major US employers to workers who are trying to unionize is a major factor in the recent decline in labor union density in the US, with the US having among the lowest union densities compared with other industrialized nations around the world.[24]

The dominant economic ideology of the 1980s, initially called "supply-side" economics, was part of corporations' battle for higher profits. This new ideology justified redistributing income and wealth from the poor to the rich as a solution to economic slowdown. The wealthy claimed they were suffering from squeezed profits and a resulting shortage of investment capital. Put another way, corporations and the rich argued they simply weren't rich enough—even while sitting on piles of money that they were not investing. The proposed remedies were: (1) increase the wealth available to corporations and the rich through higher profits and tax cuts; (2) promote corporate expansion and privatization by removing regulations; and (3) reduce government benefits to workers and welfare recipients to supposedly make them work harder.

However, it wasn't some abstract academic theory or ideology that led to financial deregulation, the abandonment of antitrust enforcement, regulations that hurt the poor, and tax changes favoring corporations and the wealthy. As with most laws and regulations, *it was the power of capitalists, their lobbyists, and their representatives in Congress* that created vast new opportunities for profit and capital accumulation. Academic theory simply shifted to justify what the wealthy wanted. The argument for cutting taxes on the wealthy and corporations went like this: these extra funds would stimulate investment, grow the economy, and create new jobs.

Corporate and right-wing foundation lobbying expanded massively in the late 1970s and 1980s. A mid-1970s Supreme Court decision (*Buckley v. Valeo*) eliminated limits on political action committee (PAC) contributions and spending. Then in 2010, the Supreme Court ruled in *Citizens United v. Federal Election Commission* that corporations and outside groups could spend unlimited funds on elections. In 2023–2024, business PACs outspent labor PACs 20 to 1. Accounting for more than an estimated 117,000 people in the greater Washington D.C. area, "lobbying has become a pernicious force in national life, courtesy of corporate America, which hugely outspends other constituencies—labor unions, consumer and environmental groups—on an enterprise now dedicated to honing ever more sophisticated methods of shaping public opinion in service of its own ends."[25]

Capital's overwhelming influence—through lobbying and direct contributions to political candidates that buy people and access to officials—has allowed it to obtain favorable laws and regulations while ensuring that unfavorable regulations are either rescinded or not enforced.

A 2023 Pew Research survey found that "80 percent of U.S. adults think that large campaign donors have too much influence on the decisions made by members of Congress, while 73 percent say the same of lobbyists and special interest groups. At the same time, 70 percent of respondents agree that the people have too little influence on what their representatives in Congress decide."[26] The final *New York Times*-Siena poll before the 2024 presidential election (late October) found that nearly two-thirds of voters said the government was "mostly working to benefit itself and the elites," rather than "the people and the country."[27] They were right. But many who voted for Trump did not understand they were simply choosing another sector of the capitalist class.

Research by Martin Gilens of Princeton University and Benjamin Page of Northwestern confirmed what many people intuitively understand: what the majority wants has little influence on what happens in Congress and government agencies. Instead, wealthy special interests largely control which laws pass and which regulations get enforced. According to Gilens and Page, organizations and lobbyists representing the wealthy and corporations "have substantial independent impacts on U.S. government policy, while average citizens and mass-based interest groups have little or no independent influence."8[7]

Many examples demonstrate this gap between what the public wants and what Congress does, especially regarding taxes on the very rich. While strong majorities believe taxes on the wealthy are too low,[29] Congress has repeatedly cut taxes on the highest earners. Missouri illustrates the disconnect between what business and the wealthy want versus what the people want. After 58 percent of Missourians voted to mandate paid sick leave for workers, the state legislature—responding to business and chamber of commerce lobbying—repealed both paid sick leave and the indexing of the minimum wage to inflation.[30] Under Trump, this corruption has reached new heights. Pay-to-play schemes and direct payments for government favors are now largely conducted in the open.[31]

Corporate power is also evident in the decades-long decline of antitrust enforcement, which has allowed companies to buy up competitors. This has produced greater industry consolidation and accelerated monopoly capitalism. [32] In key economic sectors, a small number of companies have captured large market shares, enabling them to raise prices and profits—contradicting the claim that business concentration creates more efficient production and lower prices.

A 2022 National Bureau of Economic Research (NBER) working paper titled "The Political Economy of the Decline of Antitrust Enforcement in the United States" explained how, despite receiving ample profits, companies sought to remove impediments to monopolization by reducing antitrust measures:

> [The] picture changed at the beginning of the 1970s. First, the quadrupling of oil prices in 1973 increased production costs, squeezing margins. Second, international competition dramatically intensified. Import penetration in manufacturing (the percentage of U.S. manufacturing consumption accounted by imports) rose from 5.5% in 1970 to 12.9% in 1985. Pre-tax profitability . . . which had reached a peak of 16% in 1966, averaged 9.4% in the first six years of the 1970s. Thus, American firms, especially large American firms that had dominated the world in the previous 30 years, found themselves under challenge.
>
> This decline in the relative competitiveness of large American businesses provided both a motive and an opportunity to lobby for reduced antitrust enforcement. The motive was reduced profitability.[33]

Of course, 9.4 percent pre-tax profits were hardly a serious problem. Establishment sources like the NBER downplay a key fact: monopoly capital invariably fights antitrust enforcement because it always favors higher monopoly profits—that is always the "motive" driving it. This is fundamentally a question of economic and political power. Regulatory agencies and the Supreme Court cooperated in undermining antitrust enforcement. Yet there's no evidence the public favored larger, more consolidated companies. In 1981, 79 percent of surveyed people believed that "in many of our largest industries, one or two companies have too much control of the industry."[34] The extent of concentration under monopoly capitalism is startling: At the time of the Great Financial Crisis, the top two hundred U.S. firms—out of some 5.5 million corporations, 2.0 million partnerships, 17.7 million nonfarm proprietorships, and 1.8 million farm proprietorships—accounted for about 30 percent of gross profits, and this share has been increasing. The total revenue of the top five hundred global corporations in 2008 was equivalent to some 35–40 percent of world income.[35] In most mature industries, just a few firms control most of the market.

Accelerated inflation from external shocks—such as the 1970s oil embargo or, more recently, COVID-19 pandemic supply chain disruptions—was addressed in the 1980s and 1990s through a two-stage approach. First, policymakers sharply raised interest rates to increase unemployment and quell inflation through "shock therapy." Then they gradually lowered rates over an extended period to stimulate production and finance. This approach created the conditions that led to the 2007–2009 Great Financial Crisis/Great Recession.

The Class War Continues

With Trump's second term, the war on workers has grown more virulent. According to the *Financial Times*, he "has publicly questioned the value of the federal workforce, let go thousands of government employees and ended collective bargaining for 1mn more. He is also reshaping the National Labor Relations Board, which enforces worker-protection rules, by firing its chair and adding two members that unions describe as anti-worker."[36]

Although Trump's 2025 "One Big Beautiful Bill Act" offers workers a few minor benefits (no taxes on certain tips or overtime), it has harmed many others. Fewer low-income workers can access food assistance, and many have lost Medicaid coverage. The lowest one-third of taxpayers end up with less money, while the wealthy receive the main tax benefits.

Following Trump's lead, companies have changed their approach to workers: "Not long ago, bosses routinely praised workers as their most prized asset, so much so that some hoarded new hires before having enough for them to do. Today, with a giant question mark hanging over the economy, executives are pulling no punches in saying employees need to work harder, complain less and be glad they still have jobs."[37] Companies are not only cutting workers but openly celebrating operating with less labor. As a July 2025 Wall Street Journal headline and subheading stated: "CEOs Are Shrinking Their Workforces—and They Couldn't Be Prouder: Bosses aren't just unapologetic about staff cuts. Many are touting shrinking head counts as accomplishments in the AI era."[38]

Trump's Tariffs as Part of the Class War

Claiming that other countries have been "ripping off" the United States, Trump has declared a trade war on the entire world. And tariffs on imported goods are a main part of this war. The costs of the tariffs are paid by the company that imports the goods. If companies pass along some or all of the increased costs, as is most likely, then tariffs become in effect a sales tax on the public's consumption of imported products. Moderate- and low-income workers spend a higher portion of their incomes on goods than do the wealthy. Trump maintains that the income the government receives from tariffs will substitute for the lower government income from reducing income taxes. In this way, income from tariffs helps to justify the large decrease in taxes for the wealthy. As economist Paul Krugman has written, "This supposed trade war is really a class war. Tariffs are part of a package of policies that will massively redistribute income from the have-nots to the haves."[39] Although courts have found most of Trump's initial tariffs to be illegal, little of the money returned to importers will reach the final purchasers of imported products. Meanwhile Trump's (and Netanyahu's) 2026 war on Iran caused gas, diesel, and fertilizer prices to increase drastically, resulting in significant economic pain for low- and moderate-income workers.

6

Grand Theft Capital and the Origins of the New Billionaire Economy

CAPITAL'S WAR FOR A LARGER *piece of the economic pie has been spectacularly successful.* The prolonged effort to increase their flexibility to buy other firms and increase after-tax profits has paid off for large corporations and the very wealthy. They have maintained a continuing fight against unions and their goal of obtaining better compensation and working conditions for labor. Capital's strategy also includes efforts to weaken environmental laws or their enforcement. The success in getting lower taxation rates and the very low cost of borrowing money were estimated to account for about 40 percent of the increase in real profits between 1989 and 2019.[1]

A Brief Overview of Corporate Profits

The ruling class's aggressive counteroffensive that began in the 1970s has successfully expanded profits at the expense of workers.

Corporate tax rates have decreased markedly (Figure 6.1). The effective corporate tax rate decreased from 52 percent of profits in the early 1950s to 21 percent today, in large part due to tax cuts during the Reagan, Bush, and Trump administrations. As this

Figure 6.1: Effective Corporate Tax Rate (taxes as percent of reported profits)

Sources and Notes: FRED, Series FCTAX, "Federal Government: Tax Receipts on Corporate Income" and Series CPROFIT, "Corporate Profits with Inventory Valuation Adjustment (IVA) and Capital Consumption Adjustment (CCAdj)."

occurred, the spread between reported corporate profits and the taxes paid has gotten larger, with companies keeping more of the income. The decrease in taxes contributed to a near doubling of profits as a percent of the economy from 4.4 percent of the GDP in 1995 to just over 8 percent in 2024.[2]

Not only have corporate tax rates decreased dramatically, companies have found many ways to decrease the *reported* profits and have found other ways to escape paying their fair share of taxes. U.S. corporations shifted an estimated $369 billion in profits to affiliates in low-tax countries in 2023. Globally, roughly 36 percent of all U.S. corporate profits are redirected to lower-tax jurisdictions—with the result that U.S. domestic corporate profits would have been 10 percent higher had this shifting not taken place.[3, 4] Other tax-avoidance techniques are referred to as "earnings stripping" or "debt loading," loaning money to a subsidiary in order for it to deduct interest payments.

Another key factor affecting profits that has been operating for decades is the steady concentration of economic activity through corporate consolidation. This transformed entire new sectors of the economy that had not yet experienced a shakedown process from freely competitive markets into near-monopolies or oligopolies with substantial market power. Many of these large corporations, especially the largest, have integrated both vertically—owning firms throughout their supply chains—and horizontally within their industries. Some are also conglomerates owning businesses across different industries. This concentration gives large corporations with few competitors greater power over workers, and greater ability to raise prices whenever they believe the market will bear it, helping to further increase profits.[5]

One way to measure corporate profitability is to look at "profits per unit of real gross value added"—the dollars of profit earned per dollar of GDP income created during production. This measure rose gradually after the Great Depression of the 1930s, accelerated after 2000, then surged dramatically during and after the COVID-19 disruptions (see Figure 6.2).

The inflation spike in the early 2020s had multiple causes. COVID-19 created supply-chain disruptions and economic dislocations that drove up costs. Government aid—enhanced unemployment insurance and direct payments—allowed people to save money during the pandemic while also spending more on goods. Major federal programs to combat the pandemic's economic effects, along with large Biden-era initiatives, pumped substantial money into the economy. However, a major driver of rising prices was corporate pricing power: large companies raised prices far beyond their increased costs. As prices climbed, profits per value-added jumped nearly 50 percent in just four years, rising from 15 to 22 percent (see Figure 6.2). When sellers raise prices simply because they can—even when their costs haven't increased or have increased less than their price hikes—economists call this "seller's inflation."[6]

Prices can also be increased by shrinking the amount that is

Figure 6.2: Profits Per Unit of Real Gross Value Added of Non-Financial Corporations

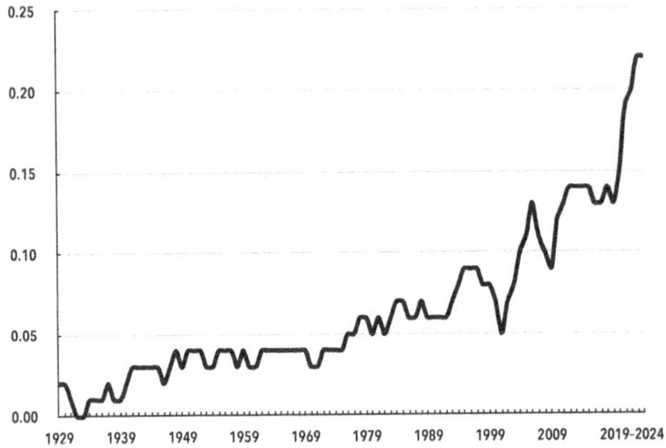

Sources and Notes: FRED, Series A463RD3A052NBEA, "Profit per unit of real gross value added of nonfinancial corporate business: Corporate profits with IVA and CCAdj (unit profits from current production), Dollars, Annual, Not Seasonally Adjusted."

sold (the weight of the contents of packaged food, for example) while not decreasing the price, a practice dubbed "shrinkflation." Another important strategy was the continuous lobbying for reductions in corporate and private taxes, thus keeping more of the profits. And reported corporate profits as a percent of the GDP—which reached 8 percent only one time in over ninety years—have averaged 9 percent since 2022.[7]

In addition to lowering corporate taxes, the wealthy successfully lobbied to slash their personal income taxes. The top marginal tax rate—the rate paid on the highest portion of income—dropped from 90 percent to 37 percent over several decades. Importantly, this 37 percent rate *applies only* to income above $600,000 for individuals (or $731,000 for couples filing jointly).

The Reagan-era justification for slashing taxes on the wealthy was economic nonsense: the claim was that giving corporations and the rich more money would stimulate investment and economic growth, with some benefits eventually "trickling down" to workers. In other words, the problem with slow growth was supposedly that the rich weren't rich enough—if they had more capital, they would invest it and grow the economy for everyone. This theory has been thoroughly discredited, yet tax cuts for the wealthy continue, often disguised as across-the-board reductions. The first Trump administration enacted massive cuts for both the wealthy and corporations through the 2017 Tax Cuts and Jobs Act. Those provisions, originally set to expire, were made permanent in the 2025 "One Big Beautiful Bill Act." The Act also includes other provisions that disproportionately benefit the wealthy, maintain low corporate tax rates, and allow companies to accelerate depreciation deductions for new investments. This accelerated depreciation has become a new tax avoidance scheme for the ultra-rich: as Bloomberg reports, tax specialists use it "to scale back what their ultrawealthy clients owe to the government," triggering "a frenzy of demand for qualifying items, from private jets to car washes and gas stations."[8]

Since there are many ways to avoid or reduce taxes actually paid, some profitable corporations pay no taxes whatsoever, while many others pay well below the stated tax code rate of 21 percent. A study of 342 corporations by the Institute on Taxation and Economic Policy found that they "paid an average effective tax rate of just 14.1%. Eighty-six companies paid an average of less than 10%; 55 of those firms paid less than 5%; and 23 corporations, including T-Mobile US and Xcel Energy, paid zero (or less) federal income tax over the five-year period—even though they made a profit each year."[9]

Of course, there was (and is) plenty of money for investment. The real problem behind slow growth in the economy is the difficulty finding enough profitable places to invest in new production of goods or services, given what is known as market saturation, or the lack of effective demand for new goods and services if produced. Thus, instead of investing in the expansion of productive capacity in the "real economy" of production, owners of money capital have increasingly focused on purchasing financial assets with the expectation of capital gains. The presence of vast quantities of cash for potential investment is indicated by the massive amounts of investment in data centers for AI in 2025–2026. However, there is the danger that firms will overinvest in relation to what the market can support, leading to the bursting of the investment and financial bubble.

At the root of current economic instability is the inequality built into the system. It has been clear for some time that the income of corporate officers has increased dramatically both in absolute terms as well as in comparison with others who work in the companies. In the 1980s it was considered that an income ratio of 10 or 12 to 1 for CEO compared to the average income in the company seemed "about right" to economists, although the ratio was actually higher. It is estimated that the CEO-to-worker ratio for the 350 largest publicly held companies increased from 21 to 1 in the 1960s to 344 to 1 in the early 2020s (see Figure 6.3).[10] When

Figure 6.3: CEO-to-Worker Compensation Ratio for the 350 Largest Publicly Owned Companies in the United States

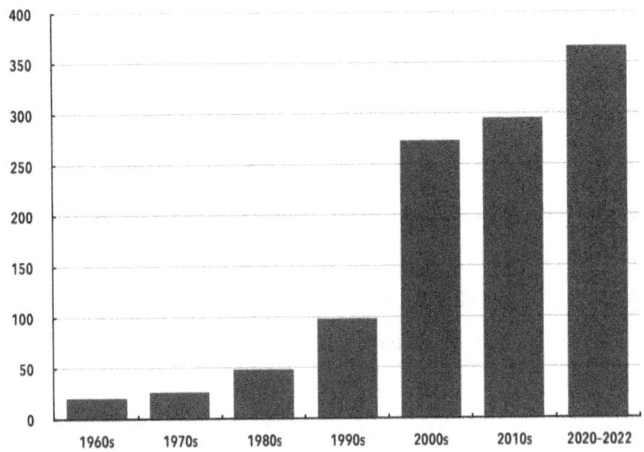

Source: Statista Research Department, "Aggregated CEO-to-worker compensation ratio for the 350 largest publicly owned companies in the United States from 1965 to 2022" (November 27, 2023). Accessed June 9, 2024, statista.com.

all compensation is taken into account, the ratio for the largest companies varies from a hundred to well over a thousand to one.[11] This means that employees would have to work hundreds to thousands of years to earn as much as the CEO earns in a single year. In 2024, the most outrageous payment for a CEO occurred when Elon Musk's $45 billion pay package was approved by Tesla stockholders. With the average Tesla worker in the United States earning $108,000 per year, Musk's 2024 pay represents a *415,000 to one CEO to worker income ratio.*

Capitalists have also succeeded in changing tax laws and using "creative" accounting to find ways around paying taxes on both business profits and their personal income: "The country's billionaires—or, more precisely, their highly compensated accountants—used deductions and exclusions, such as depreciation, to make their profitable pass-through businesses appear to be operating at a loss. Those paper losses reduced the billionaires' taxable income by $33 million a year, on average, between 2018 and 2020."[12]

Although CEO compensation increased dramatically, they still used their influence to reduce taxes, allowing them to keep a larger share of their income and wealth. Taxes were reduced on estates and income tax was cut for high earners as well as for corporations. The decrease in corporate and excise taxes meant that personal income tax would have to take up the slack. In 2022—when dedicated Social Security and Medicare taxes are omitted—personal income tax receipts represented over 70 percent of federal government tax revenue.[13] With personal income taxes becoming a larger part of federal revenue raised and high earners paying a lower percent of their income in taxes, there is more regressive tax pressure on modest earners.

That tax laws that have become more favorable to the rich is bad enough. In addition, *tax evasion* in 2019 by the richest 1 percent cost the government $163 billion, as estimated by the Treasury Department. Not only was income often underreported, but

Figure 6.4: Total Tax (Local, State, Federal) as Percent of Income

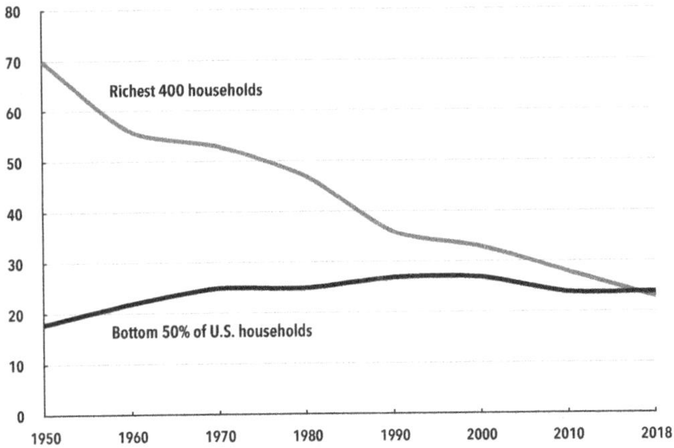

Source: Emmanuel Saez and Gabriel Zucman, *The Triumph of Injustice: How the Rich Dodge Taxes and How to Make Them Pay* (New York: W. W. Norton & Co., 2019), appendix B5.

125,000 people making more than $400,000 annually (as indicated by W-2 and 1099 tax forms), with *25,000 of those earning more than one million dollars a year, not even bothering to file tax returns between 2017 and 2021.*[14] With lawyers continually devising new ways to reduce taxes on the wealthy and the Internal Revenue Service purposefully understaffed through lobbying and unable to properly evaluate the complex tax returns of the rich, an increased burden falls especially on moderate income earners. The estate tax, which only touches the very well-off, has been a special target of lobbyists for the rich. "The [lobbying] campaign succeeded spectacularly. In 1976 about 139,000 American households were eligible for the estate tax, by 2020 it had been punctured by so many exemptions that only 1,275 households nationwide had to pay. Gary Cohn, Trump's economic adviser who helped engineer the most recent loosening of the provision, was heard to tell members of Congress, 'Only morons pay the estate tax.'"[15]

Tax law changes favoring the wealthy were so successful that the richest four hundred households are now paying lower rates of taxes (total of federal, state, and local) than those of the bottom 50 percent of households (Figure 6.4).

Income inequality has gone so far that the wealthiest 10 percent do half of all consumer spending in the economy.[16]

7

The Affordability Crisis of the Working Class

THE CLASS WAR WAGED MOSTLY by corporations and the rich has produced spectacular gains for capital and the wealthy while creating an affordability crisis for workers who face increased exploitation and economic hardship.

And the problem is only getting worse. The difference between "standard" exploitation of workers and actual expropriation or theft becomes extremely murky in low-paying jobs where workers receive so little that they are frequently eligible for government assistance with food, rent, or healthcare. These are situations in which workers are paid *less* than they need to exist. As Barbara Ehrenreich explained, superexploitation of this kind is present "when someone works for less pay than she can live on—when, for example, she goes hungry so that you can eat more cheaply, and conveniently. . . . The 'working poor,' as they are approvingly termed, are in fact the major philanthropists of our society."[1] Low-paid workers are thus also "philanthropists" to the wealthy owners of businesses, allowing them to accumulate even more capital than if the workers were paid a living wage.

In addition to clearly unfair contracts and arrangements, labor is constrained from obtaining better conditions by a pool of *potential* workers who are looking for work, even at low wages, including part-time workers wanting full-time employment.

A reserve of workers—a "reserve army" encompassing the unemployed, the underemployed, and those classified as outside the labor force who want employment—is always present, even in what seems to be a tight labor situation.[2] Although the official U.S. unemployment rate in 2024 and 2025 was lower than it had been in over fifty years—no doubt partly due to the rise in precarious contingent and independent contract workers in the digital era— workers are still entering the labor force in significant numbers, showing how little the official employment rate relates to reality.[3] This pool of potential workers allows capital to hold down wages. In addition to the officially unemployed, this pool includes all those of working age who are considered outside the labor force because they have not recently looked for work. Many of these are classified as "marginally attached" to the labor force because they are either officially listed as "discouraged" (not having sought employment in the last month) or are unable to obtain jobs because of absence of adequate transportation, lack of affordable daycare for their children, or other material reasons. There are also millions of workers who are not employed and who have expressed in the latest employment surveys that they "want a job now," but who are not categorized as marginally attached (or discouraged), since they either did not indicate that they had searched for employment in the last year, or their situation, according to the surveys, remains indeterminate. On top of all of this, still others drop out of the labor force because of the horrendous conditions of work and poor pay in most jobs. All such workers, as well as those officially unemployed, and those employed part-time wanting full-time work, properly belong to the reserve army of labor. And new immigrants—especially with the surge in 2021–2024—added significantly to the pool of potential low-wage workers. In addition, the imperial role of the United States and other rich countries allows them to draw on a massive global reserve army of labor that exceeds in size the world's active labor force.[4]

Note: There was a brief period of tight labor markets following the COVID-19 pandemic. The reasons included factors flowing from the pandemic such as early retirements and deaths, sharply reduced immigration during the pandemic, and workers dropping out due to workplace stress, job-related injuries, and illnesses. In addition, there was the further growth in this period of part-time and contract workers—the "precariat"—who are classified as employed but lack sufficient or steady work and function more as part of the reserve army of labor than members of the active workforce.

Declining labor force participation predated both the Great Recession and COVID-19 pandemic and is particularly pronounced among men without college degrees. The share of prime working-age men (25–54) either working or looking for work in the United States fell from nearly 95 percent in the late 1960s to 86 percent before the pandemic began in 2020. By 2024, 8.7 million prime working-age men were neither working nor actively seeking employment.

The Increasing Distress of the U.S. Working Class

Wealthy individuals and corporations have done extremely well over the past half-century. Profits are very strong, as can be inferred by the skyrocketing increase in profits indicated in Figure 6.2. But things are not going well for many people. Workers in the United States have had an especially difficult time over the first two decades of the twenty-first century. The first decade began with a recession following the bursting of the dot-com bubble and, after a short recovery, was soon followed by the financial and housing crisis of the Great Recession from December 2007 to June 2009.

Figure 7.1: Ratio of Median House Price to Median Family Income (10-yr. moving average)

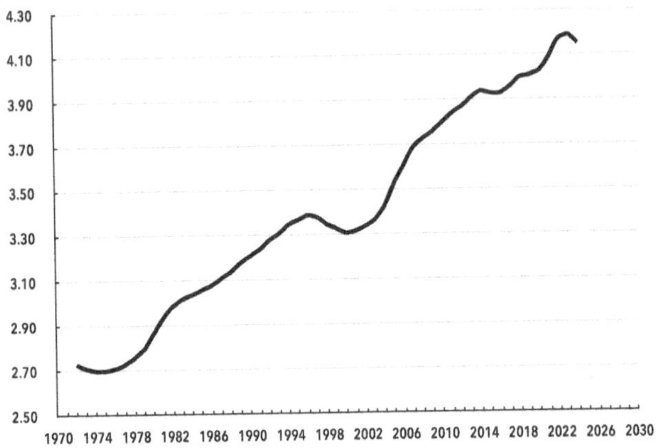

Source: FRED, Series MSPUS, "Median Sales Price of Houses Sold for the United States" and Series MEFAINUSA646N, "Median Family Income in the United States."

It took over six years for total employment to return to pre-recession levels, and even longer for the number of full-time workers to equal prerecession levels. It was nine years before the unemployment rate went down to the level before the recession, 4.7 percent. During this period, millions of people lost their homes and personal bankruptcies soared.

Housing

About two-thirds of households own their homes (with financial institutions holding mortgages on many), but home ownership is much less among minorities: Black home ownership is about 46 percent and for whites it is around 74 percent. It has become increasingly difficult for workers to purchase homes because income hasn't kept pace with the increasing price of houses (the ratio of home prices to annual income is an indicator of affordability; see Figure 7.1). In 2025, given relatively high interest rates of mortgages as well as elevated home prices and high insurance rates, even many who could afford to buy a home, decided to rent instead. A study from the Harvard Joint Center for Housing Studies found that "the annual income needed to afford monthly payments on a median-priced home in the US was $126,670 in 2024—a 60% jump from $79,330 in 2021." However, the median household income during the same period only increased by 23 percent, from $70,780 to $83,730.[5]

Rising rental prices have also made life difficult. Single-family homes represent the largest share of U.S. supply of housing units, over 80 million homes out of about 130 million total units. But about one-third of those single-family homes are being rented from individuals or corporate owners.

Home ownership rates declined from about 69 percent to 62 percent in the fallout from the Great Financial Crisis of 2007–2009, with investors buying up properties to convert to rental houses. "Investors bought at least two million homes, and almost certainly far more than that, with prices depressed. Large-scale institutional investors purchased tens of thousands of homes for less than they cost to build."[6] And during the depths of the pandemic, investors "spent billions of dollars buying homes. . . . At the 2022 peak, they bought more than one in every four single-family homes sold."[7] Wall Street firms are increasingly interested in buying to rent houses. And, according to a former Biden housing official, "When institutional investors or larger landlords own the rental units, we see an increase in the number of evictions for tenants."[8] It was estimated that in 2022 approximately 2 percent of all single-family homes in the U.S. were owned by "five of the largest investors in the United States."[9]

Investors from abroad are also buying U.S. homes and now own about 2.5 percent of U.S. houses.[10] Though not a huge percentage, it adds to the pressure on prices. And prices have increased, much more than income.

Although it is no surprise that many people cannot afford to buy a home, those that already have houses are finding it difficult to maintain their mortgaged homes in the climate of inflating costs for property tax, insurance, increased mortgage payments (if they have a variable rate mortgage), and increased utility costs, while other costs such as food are increasing as well. As a Maine resident put it, "It's completely overwhelming. I feel trapped."[11]

Corporate and small private investors continue to drive up prices of rentals as well as home purchases. A 2023 report on the Greater Boston area found that "highly capitalized investors and cash buyers are taking over a significant share of the market and pushing out more traditional and non-profit buyers."[12] Institutional investors bought approximately 20 percent of houses sold in the area from 2004 to 2018.

Builders are constructing more expensive and profitable larger homes rather than what used to be called "starter" houses. Median home size has increased about 60 percent since the 1960s as the typical household has shrunk by 25 percent. The situation in the Denver area is such that you can't "buy those Denver area homes built 25 years ago at an entry-level price today, either. They go for half a million dollars."[13]

In a number of urban areas, U.S. companies have also overbuilt high-end rental apartments (about 400,000 to 600,000 4- and 5-star units, according to the lingo, under construction) while building few small and lower-rent apartments (3,000 to 7,000 1- and 2-star apartment units under construction).[14]

Also affecting the availability and affordability of the home purchase/rental market are the approximately 10 million second homes and the roughly 0.6 million short-duration rental units available on Airbnb.

About one-third of all households rent apartments or houses. Skyrocketing rents along with inflation in other parts of the economy, including the rising cost of food, have been disastrous for literally millions of people. A common rule of thumb is that renters should pay no more than one-third of their income on rent. This

Table 7.1:Income Share Paid in Rent and Utilities (2022)

Income	Rent as percent of income
Under $15,000	85
15,000 to 29,999	82
30,000 to 49,999	67
45,000 to 74,999	41
75,000 and up	11

Source: **America's Rental Housing 2024,** Joint Center for Housing Studies of Harvard Univer-sity, accessed February 18, 2024 at https://www.jchs.harvard.edu/sites/default/files/reports/files/Harvard_JCHS_Americas_Rental_Housing_2024.pdf.

would supposedly leave sufficient income for all other needs—food, education, transportation, clothing, etc. But an estimated 22 million households—about half of all renters—spend greater than 30 percent of their income on rent, while for the low-income population it can be half or more of their income. (Table 7.1).

The majority of renters feel that their rent is so high it keeps them from getting ahead economically, that things are barely livable for them and that the "dream" of owning their own home is dead.[15] Unable to pay rent when it's due, many tenants turn to credit cards, which trigger additional landlord fees, or buy-now, pay-later services offering two-week loans at costs exceeding 100 percent annually.[16]

The rental/home purchase crisis of the early- to mid-2020s is, as conventional economists might call it, a market failure. The construction of housing has not kept up with the needs of the population. By 2023 the housing market was estimated to need an extra 6.5 million units.[17] Relying on the wonders of the so-called free market is not sufficient to provide decent housing—nor a good diet or adequate healthcare and so on—for everyone. While local zoning regulations may to a certain extent slow down building new dwellings, the decision of what to build in a given location and whether to build at all is up to the real estate and construction industries. And while giveaways (property tax rebates, for example) play a role, these decisions are based on whether financial conditions (costs of land, material, and labor relative to selling/rental price) will result in the rate of profits they want. The decision on whether or not to build is *not* based on the needs of the population. The huge climate-related disasters—hurricanes, floods, wildfires—have created the need for many new or significantly repaired homes.

Problems of insufficient income relative to all expenses causes people to skimp on necessities such as food. And with capital spending for municipal waterworks declining and many low-income families living in substandard housing or unable to pay for all their utilities, "plumbing poverty" has increased in urban areas. A 2025 Bloomberg article was titled "Why Access to Running Water Is a Luxury in Wealthy US Cities."[18]

Like other aspects of the economy, concentration of ownership has occurred in the construction industry. Although there are approximately 60,000 developers in the United States, only twenty-five accounted for beginning construction on 25 percent of the multi-family housing units being built in 2022.[19] And with regard to construction of single-family homes, according to the National Association of Home Builders, in 1989 the top 10 builders captured 8.7 percent of closings; in 2022 it was 43.2 percent.[20]

Construction of new housing units relative to population had been declining in the period between the 1980s and the early twenty-first century housing mania that preceded the Great Financial Crisis of 2007–2009 (Figure 7.2). During the pre-Crisis period, people were buying houses for speculative purposes. Following the housing boom and the Great Recession, home building declined even more rapidly until the late 2010s. Trump's deportation program means that building housing is becoming more difficult. With immigrants accounting for about 30 percent of workers in the construction industry—over 50 percent in four

Figure 7.2: Thousands of Housing Unit Starts per Million Households (10-yr. moving average)

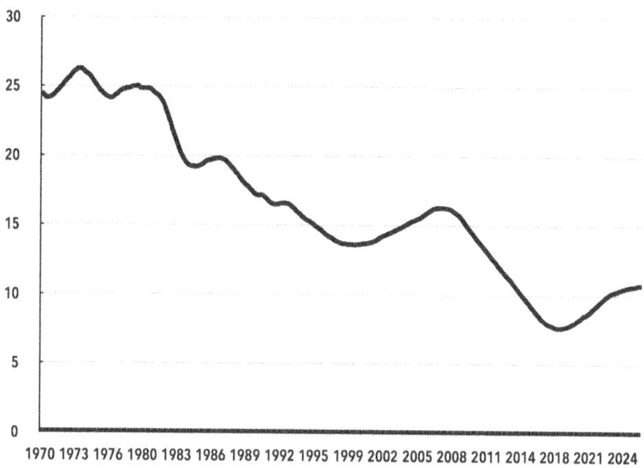

Source: FRED, Series TTLHHM156N, "Household Estimates" and Series HOUST, "New Privately-Owned Housing Units Started: Total Units."

states—it is not clear who will replace immigrant labor. With the decline of unions in the industry "construction jobs became less desirable, as eroding wages and working conditions diminished the quality and job security of the profession. Only then did immigrants, with the encouragement of the political and business class, fill a gap that was already opening."[21]

The best way to deal with our housing crisis—where the problem is *affordability* in addition to the sheer number of new units needed—is *not* to rely on the real estate construction industry and the "free market." Instead, social housing, built by governments or nonprofits for the purpose of housing people with a range of incomes, including those with low incomes, can provide good housing at modest prices.[22] Stagnating wages together with increasing prices make for a difficult existence for many people. And it is important to keep in mind that, because of racism, minority workers have more difficulties than white workers. The unemployment rate of Black workers is usually about twice that of whites.

Transportation

Many workers live some distance from their work, due to the higher cost of housing in urban areas. The absence of reliable public transportation means that they are reliant on their cars, with approximately 75 percent of workers driving to work. However, automobiles have become much more expensive to purchase and own. In addition to the large increase in price, costs have increased dramatically for insurance and repair. The average *annual cost of car ownership* of a new car is estimated between 9 and 12 thousand dollars.[23] As the price of a new car has risen, so have the prices of used vehicles. And, while car loans lasting four or five years were common, now seven-year loans are needed to manage monthly payments.[24] Auto loan delinquencies have increased dramatically over the 2020s. The large increase in gas prices during Trump's 2026 war with Iran has added another burden to commuting.

Debt

Mortgage debt once far exceeded other forms of household debt, such as for healthcare, credit cards, student loans, and auto loans. A largely hidden and growing source of indebtedness is the buy-now, pay-later system; more than half of its users report that it led them to spend more than they could afford.[25] By 2024, total interest paid on non-mortgage debt was roughly equal to interest paid on home mortgages.[26] Although overall household debt has risen substantially, it still remains below the level—relative to disposable income—that prevailed just before the 2007–2009 Great Financial Crisis.

Childcare and Helping Older Children

Childcare is a critical service for single parents and for two-parent households in which both parents hold paying jobs. The childcare industry had been on the brink of collapse for decades even before the COVID-19 pandemic worsened the problem.

> There is a reason that in 2021, Treasury Secretary Janet Yellen described the child care market as a failure. A 2020 report from the left-leaning Center for American Progress estimated that before the pandemic, there were "more than four children under age 3 per licensed child care slot, or enough licensed child care to serve just 23 percent of infants and toddlers," and found that 80 percent of counties in its study "would be classified as an infant and toddler child care desert."[27]

Following the end of COVID-era assistance from the federal government, childcare centers have closed at a rapid rate, frequently with little notice.

Another form of stress is that with the cost of living so high, about half of U.S parents are financially assisting their grown children, many of whom have student loans to pay off, providing a place to stay (or helping to pay for rental/mortgage), and helping to pay bills for such expenses as cell phones and food.[28]

Someone defending the current economic system might view widespread homelessness and hunger in a wealthy country as a specific market failure that needs targeted fixes. Additionally, they might argue that the poor are responsible for their own poverty and it is up to them to do something about it. However, this perspective overlooks how these problems stem from capitalism's core function: producing goods and services to maximize profit—which includes minimizing wages—rather than to meet human needs.

Labor's Wages and Working Conditions

The war on workers' wages and working conditions has only accelerated. In addition to routine exploitation, there are a number of ways that firms cut workers' wages. One is to avoid paying overtime (at 50 percent more than base wages) through job title inflation, which means creating position titles that make it appear as if a worker is a manager. When a front desk clerk becomes a "director of first impressions," a barber becomes a "grooming manager," or a food cart attendant becomes a "food cart manager," workers do not come under mandatory extra pay for overtime.[29] Still another way for companies to avoid paying overtime—or, for that matter, sometimes even any defined wage or other compensation—is to classify workers as independent contractors instead of employees.

One ploy to suppress wages is for businesses to contract out a portion of needed labor—custodial work, for example—to other companies that employ workers at low wages, with no healthcare or pension coverage. In addition to companies saving on labor costs, subcontractors are blamed when there are problems such as illegally exploiting migrant child labor to perform dangerous tasks.[30] A report by the Economic Policy Institute found that "since 2021, 28 states have introduced bills to weaken child labor laws, and 12 states have enacted them."[31]

A fairly new way of heightening the exploitation of workers takes the form of *noncompete clauses*. It is estimated that nearly 20 percent of the private labor force has been required to promise not to leave the job and go to another company doing the same or similar work.[32] These noncompete clauses help to depress wages and to introduce worse work conditions by making it difficult for workers to change jobs and therefore to move to where wages and working conditions are better. Other techniques for controlling and exploiting labor include: (1) a requirement of some workers to give four months' notice or face paying the business for leaving before that period; (2) requiring the workers to pay a company for the training received when they leave; and (3) forcing foreign workers to pay an exorbitant fee for leaving. Health Carousel LLC, for example, charges "a $20,000 quitting fee to coerce foreign nurses into remaining in miserable working conditions."[33]

Then there is the actual direct theft of wages by capital. It is estimated that U.S. workers are robbed of some $50 billion annually.[34] This type of expropriation includes not paying for overtime, paying less than the minimum wage, compelling workers to work longer hours than they are paid for, and stealing tips. According to an article in *Forbes Advisor*, "low-wage workers, in industries such as construction, child care and food services, are disproportionately affected by wage theft."[35]

Rampant exploitation and robbery of workers exist in the poultry and meat processing industries. This includes illegally using child labor (mostly immigrant), having them work long hours in dangerous jobs, and not paying overtime. For example, a U.S. Department of Labor 2023 investigation "found the company [The Exclusive Poultry Inc.] endangered young workers recklessly in Southern California . . . [and] in addition to their unlawful employment of children and retaliation against workers, the employers failed to pay workers their required wages."[36] The company supplies poultry to supermarkets and distributors such as Sysco. Fines for safety violations, including when child workers (or others) are killed, are not sufficiently high to stop the unsafe conditions. Penalties become just another cost of doing business.

One technique often used by capital to increase profits through higher rates of labor exploitation is to cut staff jobs below the actual number needed to carry out tasks safely and without exceptional stress. This leaves the remaining workers scrambling and constantly under pressure. This has happened in many sectors, such as for-profit hospitals and nursing homes and in warehouses. Staffing of railroads has decreased so greatly that it is hard for workers to take a sick day or to make medical appointments: "Even as railroads are operating longer and longer freight trains that sometimes stretch for miles, the companies have drastically reduced staffing levels, prompting unions to warn that moves meant to increase profits could endanger safety and even result in disasters."[37]

More than 22 percent of the jobs at railroads Union Pacific, CSX, and Norfolk Southern have been eliminated since 2017, when CSX implemented a cost-cutting system called Precision Scheduled Railroading which most other U.S. railroads later copied. BNSF, the largest U.S. railroad and the only one that hasn't expressly adopted that model, has still made staff cuts to improve efficiency and remain competitive.[38]

Staff cuts have real-world effects on workers and the general public. In late 2022, as Congress and the Biden administration rushed to forestall a national railroad strike, they neglected the workers' concerns about difficult conditions caused by short staffing: "Railroad workers had pushed for paid sick days to provide relief for grueling schedules caused by . . . labor cuts, with many workers on call 24/7 every day of the year, often having to work while sick or forgo doctor's appointments because of their scheduling demands and strict disciplinary policies around attendance."[39] In addition to "precision scheduling systems" that cut railroad crews, companies also skimped on maintenance. This corporate negligence possibly played a role in the February 2023 derailment in Ohio of rail cars that burned and released a variety of very toxic materials. According to Leo McCann, chair of the rail labor division of the AFL-CIO's transportation trades department: "The railroads are more interested in profitability and keeping their return on investment up and their numbers down so they can satisfy Wall Street, and they just live behind this shield hoping nothing will happen."[40]

Workers face increasing hardship due to "deindustrialization," the widespread loss of industrial jobs across the United States. This isn't simply about losing well-paying, unionized manufacturing jobs. Entire communities and even cities have been hollowed out as their economic foundations disappeared. Three main forces drive this process: increased automation and robotization, the relocation of factories to the nonunion southern United States, and international trade agreements that encourage companies to move production overseas.

The international "free trade" agreements have accelerated a broader pattern in which U.S. multinational corporations practice "global labor arbitrage"—exploiting workers in the Global South by shifting production to countries where wages are dramatically lower than in the United States, even when accounting for differences in productivity.[41] These countries also typically have weaker environmental regulations and faster permitting processes, which further boost corporate profits. This global system persists because it's supported by the economic, political, and military structures of imperialism, with the United States at its center.

Global labor arbitrage has produced a worldwide race to the bottom in wages, moving production to countries with lower unit labor costs. And if wages increase relative to productivity in these locations, companies may move production to countries with even lower unit labor costs. This leads to deepening economic insecurity and hardship for people across much of the capitalist world economy. In the United States, this dynamic has contributed to an epidemic of "deaths of despair." It is important to note, however, that chronic despair has long been present in Black communities, rooted in persistently high unemployment, low-wage work, and pervasive discrimination across all areas of life. The issue gained sustained mainstream attention only after similar conditions spread into white communities.[42]

Profiting from Poverty

Beyond poverty wages, poor and low-income workers are subject to additional forms of expropriation. Housing rents are high relative to the quality and value of the dwellings and have risen rapidly over the past decade. The *New York Times* reports "landlords operating in poor neighborhoods typically earn profits that are roughly double those of landlords in affluent communities."[43] Because they have little or no savings, low-income workers pay a large share of the roughly $11 billion collected each year in bank overdraft fees. Those without access to the formal banking system pay about $1.6 billion in check-cashing fees and $9 billion in payday-loan fees. Today, payday loans are often accessed electronically through what is known as Earned Pay Access. The interest and fees on these short-term loans commonly amount to the equivalent of a *391 percent annual rate*. During heatwaves, the need for extra cash to pay for cooling drives even greater reliance on these short-term, high-cost loans. And now you can obtain personal loans nearly instantly from online "expedited funding" companies that also charge high interest rates.

A relatively new method of extracting money from minority communities is the spread of Bitcoin ATMs, or BTMs. A Bloomberg headline made their function explicit: "Bitcoin ATMs Flood Black, Latino Areas, Charging Fees up to 22%."[44] These machines allow users to insert cash to purchase Bitcoin while charging high fees, but they generally do not allow users to withdraw cash. To convert Bitcoin back into dollars, users must go elsewhere and pay additional fees. Although BTMs are often justified as expanding financial inclusion for low-income populations, they do so in a highly exploitative manner.

Given the relatively high rents paid by low-income households, along with the spread of buy-now, pay-later schemes, payday loans, BTMs, and other high-cost services it is clear—as counterintuitive as it may be—that there is real money to be made off the poor.[45]

Dangerous Workplaces

Many workplaces are not safe. Fifty years after the passage of the Occupational Safety and Health Act in 1970,

> too many workers remain at serious risk of injury, illness or death

> as chemical plant explosions, major fires, construction collapses, infectious disease outbreaks, workplace assaults and other preventable workplace tragedies continue to occur. Workplace hazards kill and disable approximately 125,000 workers each year—4,764 from traumatic injuries and an estimated 120,000 from occupational diseases. Job injury and illness numbers continue to be severe undercounts of the real problem.[46]

With nearly one million workers, Amazon is the second-largest private employer in the country. After many years of complaints of injuries in their warehouses, internal corporate documents indicated that "Amazon itself had documented the link between its quotas [to push workers harder] and elevated injury rates."[47]

The AFL-CIO 2022 report on worker safety and health in the United States summarized the damage done annually for the period 2001 to 2022:

- 340 workers died each day from hazardous working conditions.
- 4,764 workers were killed on the job in the United States.
- An estimated 120,000 workers died from occupational diseases.
- The job fatality rate was 3.4 per 100,000 workers.
- Latino and Black workers remain at greater risk of dying on the job than all workers.
- Employers reported nearly 3.2 million work-related injuries and illnesses.
- Musculoskeletal disorders continue to make up the largest portion (21 percent) of work-related injuries and illnesses.
- Underreporting is widespread—the true toll of work-related injuries and illnesses is 5.4 million to 8.1 million each year.[48]

The greatest number of deaths each year, about 1,000, is in the construction industry, which also has exceptionally high numbers of suicides among workers.[49] The occupation with the highest *rate* of deaths is logging, with about 100 logger deaths annually for 100,000 workers. The most dangerous *workplace* in the United States is in Alabama: "At Phenix Lumber Co., workers had lost fingers, broken bones and been mangled by machines—at least 28 employees had reported injuries since 2010, at a company with only about 50 people on the payroll at a time. Three had died. A medical examiner's report detailed how just 23 pounds of one employee was recovered after he was caught in a machine. It had reached the point, some former workers said, that they would pray before the start of their $9-an-hour shifts."[50] Despite millions in OSHA fines, the agency can't shut down unsafe worksites. City fire code violations forced Phenix Lumber into filing for bankruptcy in 2023, with a trial set for 2026.

As the climate changes and more hot days and nights occur, outdoor workers need more breaks out of the sun and regular access to clean water. This is not an issue of comfort: workers have suffered significant damage to their health, including death, as a result of heatstroke. The headline of a *Guardian* story described it: "You feel like you're suffocating . . . Florida outdoor workers are collapsing in the heat without water and shade."[51] Dade County, Florida, was on the verge of passing an ordinance "to mandate employers to provide 10 minutes of rest every two hours, access to clean, cool water, and shade when temperatures hit 95F (35C)." Despite its hot and humid summers, the governor and legislature, in response to intense lobbying by business, has made it impossible for localities to set mandatory standards for humane conditions for the state's estimated 1.8 million outdoor workers. Federal regulations call for access to water, but there may not be enough for the workday. The Environmental Protection Agency estimates that, from 1992 to 2022, about 34 workers died each year from exposure to heat.[52] On the other hand, a 2024 report from Public Citizen estimates annual heat-related deaths of workers at 2,000, with 170,000 injured.[53]

Although regulations once kept certain occupational diseases at a low level, lack of enforcement or updates have caused irreparable harm to workers. One of the worst has been the return of black lung disease among coal miners. Black lung, caused by inhaling too much coal dust (or a mix of coal dust and quartz or sandstone rock dust), essentially disappeared as mine air-quality regulations were enforced. It has now returned with a vengeance, debilitating many workers and leading to premature deaths.[54] Workers trying to slow down or stop the spread of wild fires have not been warned of the health consequences, especially when not wearing respirators. Frequent exposure to fire smoke and ash can result in lung cancer, respiratory diseases, and heart problems.[55] In addition, most are poorly paid.

Worker Discontent

When low wages, unpleasant, difficult or dangerous working conditions, the high cost of housing and food relative to income, and problems accessing healthcare are added together, it is understandable that many people are in distress. The results of a 2023 survey of 2,000 U.S. workers by Alight, a workforce consulting company, indicates that about one-third of workers often dread going to work. Frequently they don't get enough hours of work, forcing them to look for other jobs to supplement income. Other results are also stark:

> The study reveals employee well-being has remained relatively stagnant over the past year, with only half (51%) of the workforce reporting positive feelings across their mental, physical and financial well-being in 2023, compared to 53% of employees in 2022. Notably, less than half of employees (41%) believe their employer cares about their well-being—a six-percentage point decline year-over-year—and just 56% of employees say they feel in control of their well-being . . .
>
> The study shows three-quarters of U.S. employees report they are experiencing moderate to high stress levels, rising to 80% among Gen Z and Millennial workers. Personal finances (56%),

job challenges (52%) and physical health (32%) rank as the top three sources of stress, while 29% of employees say their mental health has declined due to the current economic environment.

Meanwhile, 75% of workers report experiencing some adverse effect of job-related stress, with sleep disruption (53%), low morale (43%) and anxiety attacks (37%) having the biggest impacts. Nearly one-third (30%) of workers believe their job negatively impacts their mental health. . . .

Thirty-one percent of workers report feeling financial stress and often have no money left over at the end of the month. This is despite taking actions such as reducing their spending, which more than two-thirds (67%) have done. Additionally, nearly half (49%) of employees are concerned the money they have won't last, 46% feel their finances control their life and 39% fear they will never have the life they desire due to their finances. . . .

When U.S. employees need to see a doctor, many cannot access one. Almost half (47%) say they have been unable to receive services like doctor visits, lab work, urgent care, specialist care or surgeries when required.

Of those that did not or could not seek healthcare, 41% attribute it to costs, 23% were unsure where to go and 23% faced long wait times. Plus, 38% say they had problems trusting their doctor, often due to a lack of time spent with them.[56]

Inadequate Social Safety Net and Worker Pay

The United States has an extremely deficient safety net for helping low- to moderate-income workers. Millions of people have no health insurance while millions of others have inadequate insurance. Although Medicaid expanded during the height of the COVID-19 pandemic—when states were forbidden to remove people from the rolls—some 19 million were forced out of the program from the spring of 2023 to early 2024.[57] Other COVID-19–era programs that reduced poverty, hunger, homelessness, etc., have now been rescinded. From about 800,000 to a few million people are homeless (depending on how they are counted), although the country has sufficient resources to build good housing for all. Around 40 million are considered to be "food insecure" and not adequately nourished in the midst of a bounty of agricultural production.

With the sparse social safety net, U.S. workers understandably fear losing their jobs. When an earner in a family of four loses a job, unemployment benefits cover about 36 percent of the earnings when employed. Thus, families can quickly fall behind in paying all their expenses. A family of the same size in Sweden would receive 90 percent of their wages when unemployed for a similar time.[58]

The plight of working people has gotten so severe that it is even discussed in the mainstream business press. At the end of 2020, during the COVID-19 pandemic, the *Financial Times* published an editorial outlining some of the problems in the United States and other rich economies:

> Most of us depend—at times literally for our lives—on people stocking shelves, delivering food, cleaning hospitals, caring for the old and infirm. Yet many of these unsung heroes are underpaid, overworked, and suffer unpredictable work opportunities and insecurity while on the job. A neologism coined to describe them—the "precariat"—is apt. . . . The epidemic of low-paid, insecure jobs reflects a failure. . . . Over the past four decades, work has failed to secure stable and adequate incomes for growing numbers of people. This shows up in stagnant wages, erratic incomes, non-existent financial buffers for emergencies, low job security and brutalised working conditions. . . . Many suffer a rising risk of homelessness and epidemics of drug and alcohol-related diseases. Benefit systems can help—but can also trap already vulnerable people in labyrinthine administrative Catch-22s.[59]

As capital has gotten a larger slice of the pie, the share going to workers has decreased. The government collects information for all workers in the private sector and separately for the subgroup referred to as "production and non-supervisory" workers. This category comprises about 80 percent of all workers in private business, or about 100 million employees. From the 1950s through the mid-'70s, average "real compensation" (wages plus fringe benefits, corrected for inflation) of production and non-supervisory workers increased in line somewhat with increased GDP and productivity, approximately doubling. But over the last four decades, while real per capita GDP doubled again, real median compensation increased by about 28 percent and the real median weekly earnings of wage and salary workers—as estimated by the Consumer Price Index (CPI)—increased by a meager 11 percent between the late 1970s and early 2020s (Figure 7.3).[60]

Figure 7.3: Real per Capita GDP, Real Average Hourly Compensation of Production and Non-Supervisory Workers, and Real Median Weekly Earnings of Wage and Salary Workers

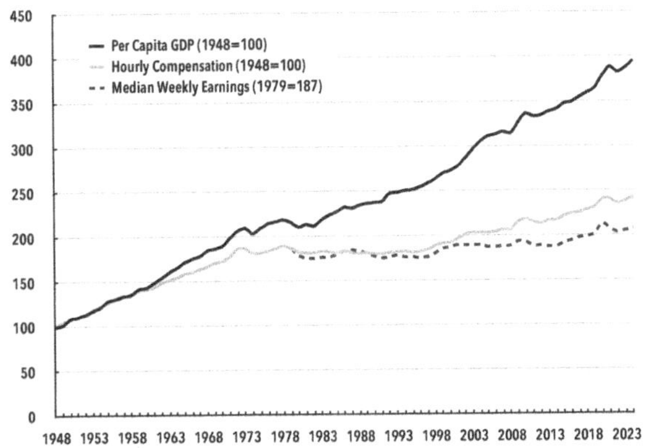

Sources and Notes: *Per Capita GDP*: FRED, Series A939RX0Q048SBEA, "Real gross domestic product per capita"; *Hourly Compensation*: Economic Policy Institute, Working America Data Library, "Productivity and Hourly Compensation," epi.org, updated September 2021. All three data series are plotted as index values; *Median Weekly Earnings*: Series LES1252881600Q, "Employed full time: Median usual weekly real earnings: Wage and salary workers: 16 years and over." The index of real median weekly earnings begins in 1979, the first year in which data is available, with 1979=187.

Figure 7.4: Weekly Earnings Adjusted for Inflation Using the Consumer Price Index (CPI) and the True Living Cost (TLC)

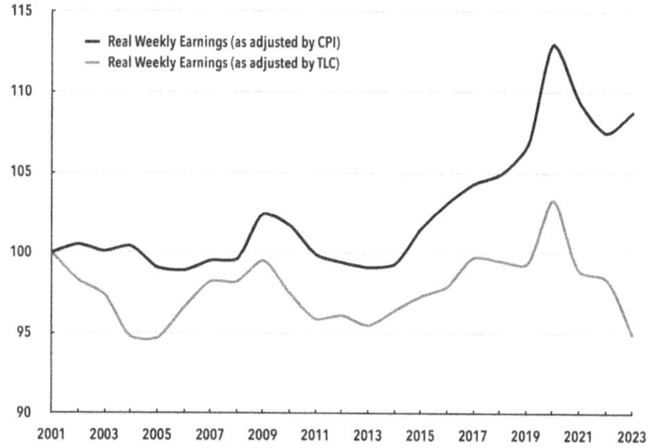

Source: Ludwig Institute for Shared Economic Prosperity. Accessed September 22, 2025 at https://www.lisep.org/tlc.

Solving the Mystery: Inflation Effects on Workers Are Worse Than Official Figures Indicate

As shown in Figure 7.3, real median weekly earnings appear to have increased, though very slowly compared to economic growth. If that is really so, then why are so many people struggling to get by? When the Bureau of Economic Statistics estimates the effects of inflation on income, the Consumer Price Index (CPI) is calculated for urban populations. It assumes a particular mix of purchases and is used to calculate changes in "real" (inflation corrected) income or production over the years. But Gene Ludwig, U.S. comptroller of the currency under President Bill Clinton, and others at the Ludwig Institute for Shared Economic Prosperity find the calculations to be misleading. In critiquing the CPI, Ludwig maintains: "The CPI is not tremendously relevant to the lived experience of middle- and low-income Americans who don't buy 80,000 goods and services. . . . If we're going to have a number that is relevant to them, it's got to be a smaller group of items that matter to their lives."[61] Using alternative measures of inflation—such as actual rent costs instead of estimates of housing expenses, using insurance premiums and other out-of-pocket costs when calculating medical expenses, etc.—that reflect actual purchases of moderate- and low-income families, is a better way to account for inflation effects on wages. For example, the Institute estimates that from 2022 to 2023 the increase in the price of basic necessities for moderate- and low-income families was 9.4 percent, more than double the "official" increase in the CPI estimate of 4.1 percent. Weighting the increasing costs differently over the last twenty years leads to starkly different conclusions (see Figure 7.4). *While the CPI increased by nearly 90 percent between 2001 and 2023, the True Living Cost (TLC) estimate of inflation increased by 131 percent.*[62] The modest increase in wages (inflation adjusted using CPI) disappears and becomes an actual loss of purchasing power when utilizing the changes in prices of what modest- and low-income families actually purchase (using the TLC). In general, when considering what people actually purchase with their disposable income, the inflation effects on the bottom 10 percent of earners is worse than the next 10 percent, which is more than the next 10 percent and so on.[63]

Labor's Share

With profits increasing as income of workers stagnates it should come as no surprise that labor's share of the national income (GDP) has declined with workers compensation now accounting for about 52 percent of the GDP. When considering the wages of production and non-supervisory workers in private employment, the decline was about one-third, from about 30 percent to around 20 percent of GDP (Figure 7.5). A much smaller share of income or value added in the economy was therefore going to wages, especially for those earning lower incomes. The inverse of this is that a larger share of value added was being appropriated by capital, resulting in enormous capital surpluses amassed at the top of the economy.

Companies use large portions of their profits for buying their

Figure 7.5: Total Annual Earnings of Production and Non-Supervisory Workers as a Percent of GDP

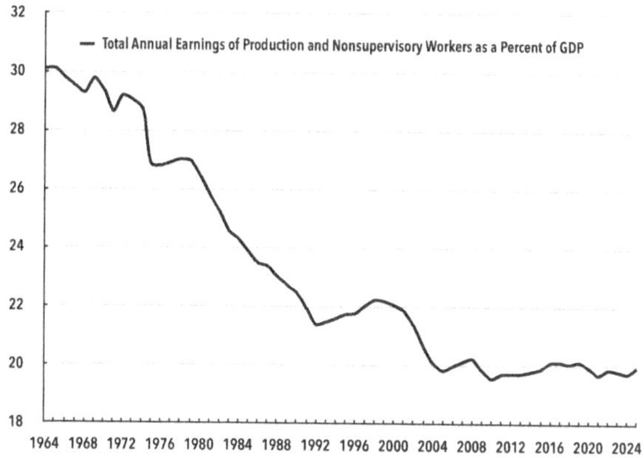

Sources and Notes: FRED Series CES0500000030, "Average Weekly Earnings of Production and Nonsupervisory Employees, Total Private," Series CES0500000006, "Production and Non-supervisory Employees, Total Private," and Series GDP, "Gross Domestic Product." Accessed May 6, 2024.

own stock or to pay dividends and *still* accumulate piles of cash that aren't used for investment purposes. In 2026, non-financial corporations were sitting on 8 trillion dollars in total liquidity (easily available assets) that were not being invested in production (much of it stashed abroad to avoid taxes), a phenomenon characteristic of monopoly-finance capital, where the economy is geared more to amassing financial assets and hoarding cash than to productive investment.[64] The "liquidity" (or cash equivalents) is not just sitting there, of course. Much is stored in money market funds or other interest-bearing liquid assets instead of being used to expand production.

A *Wall Street Journal* article on the issue begins as follows: "Having more money than you know what to do with used to be a high-quality problem. Now it is just a problem." It continues: "The largest tech companies in the world are also the richest. Apple, Amazon and the parent companies of Google and Facebook META now collectively sit on a little more than

$570 billion in cash, short-term and long-term investments. That is more than double the collective pile of the next five richest non-financial companies on the S&P 500 index, according to data from S&P Global Market Intelligence."[65] (This pile of cash allowed companies in 2025 to quickly invest in the rush to build data centers to service the projected future demands from AI use.) Even manufacturing companies had large amounts of excess cash at the end of 2025, with around $600 billion on hand.[66]

It is estimated that the large companies in the S&P 500 index used $795 billion in 2023 (down from nearly $1 trillion in 2022) to buy their own stock in order to prop up prices.[67] In early 2024,

AVERAGE (MEAN) vs. MEDIAN

Most people are accustomed to using and reading about numerical averages. To get the average (mean) you sum up a list and divide by the number present. For example: the sum of 5, 10, 20, 40, and 100 equals 175 and the average is 175/5 or 35. The median, on the other hand, represents the value in the middle, with half below and half above; in this case it is 20. Notice the difference between the average (35) and the median (20). The average is quite a bit higher than the median, because of the one 100. If these were salaries and the units were in thousands of dollars, the average would be $35,000 while the median would be only $20,000. If we want to know how people in the middle are doing with respect to income, the median portrays it better than the mean. In the real world some extremely high incomes produce an average much higher than the median income. The median numbers for a statistical series are usually not readily available and there is no choice but to use averages. In the charts in this book we use median values when available and averages when they are not.

Sometimes, the use of averages is preferred. For example, the total income of a group of people can be estimated by using average income multiplied by the number of people in the group (for example, see Figure 7.5).

Meta and Apple used tens of billions of dollars from their pile of cash to repurchase stock. For the entire year of 2024, $945 billion were used for stock buybacks by the S&P 500 companies: *"more than 50% higher than aggregate business investment in research and development."*[68] In 1982 the Securities and Exchange Commission legalized the use of profits to purchase a company's own stock. Since then, a significant portion of profits that in the past would have gone to the research labs of major corporations such as IBM, Xerox, GE, and DuPont began to be used for stock buybacks. Although another theoretically possible use for profits is to pay workers higher wages, that never seems to happen. And venture capital is presented with the same problem as non-financial companies, not able to find sufficient new companies to absorb their estimated $300 billion of "dry powder" (cash).[69]

When corporations are flush, wage stagnation for the working class has profound negative effects. For example, it is estimated that male workers over twenty-five years old and earning the median wage in 1985 had to work full-time for forty weeks to afford a year of a so-called middle-class life, using a "Cost-of-Thriving Index" first established by the Manhattan Institute, depicting the standard necessary for sustained living at a "middle-class" level (including "middle-class essentials of a comfortable house, a car, healthcare, and education"). Today, because the median real wage (inflation corrected) has actually fallen, it takes a full sixty-two weeks (more than the weeks in a year) to generate the same standard of living. This means either working multiple jobs or having a two-earner household is essential to reaching this income level. For that portion of men over twenty-five who only have a high school education, the working time it takes to attain this living standard for a year went from about forty-three weeks in 1985 to eighty weeks in 2022.[70] When it is considered that half of all workers by definition earn less than the median wage (or median compensation), it is no surprise that so many people are struggling today. *Over 60 percent of workers (even half of those earning $100,000 or more) are* *living paycheck-to-paycheck, with few or no reserves available if an unexpected emergency occurs.*[71]

Inadequate Retirement Funding

With so many workers living paycheck-to-paycheck and struggling to get by, it's no surprise that most people lack adequate retirement savings. In 2017, the U.S. Census Bureau found that "49% of adults ages 55 to 66 had no personal retirement savings."[72] This problem stems partially from a shift in how companies provide retirement benefits. Pensions—in which employers contribute to a fund and manage it, and guarantee benefits in retirement—were once common in private business, with over 60 percent of private sector workers covered by one in 1980. But in a move to shift the cost and risk to workers, companies shifted to "defined contribution" plans, referred to as a 401(k) accounts in the tax code. In such plans, workers contribute all or the larger share of contributions to a number of investment funds. The popularity of defined contribution plans for businesses instead of the traditional pensions is clear: they are cheaper for the companies. The proportion of private sector workers participating in defined benefit plans fell to 11 percent in 2022.[73] And while many workers are enrolled in 401(k) plans, it turns out that there are many problems, such as the hidden fees that various funds subtract.

The Full Magnitude of the Robbery of the Working Class

Over recent decades, as we have seen, legal and regulatory changes have enabled corporations and wealthy individuals to expand their assets dramatically while constraints on wage growth have caused real wages for most workers to stagnate. The actual purchasing power of workers' wages has remained flat since the 1970s.[74] Moreover, using the Consumer Price Index (CPI) to cor-

Table 7.2: Pre-Tax Income and Difference between Equitable and Actual Income Increases, 1980–2018

Income percent range	Pre-tax 2018 income (dollars)	Difference between equitable and actual income increases (dollars)
0-10	11,113	8,746
10-20	17,557	11,195
20-30	24,463	13,968
30-40	32,439	15,558
40-50	42,182	15,439
50-60	53,344	14,581
60-70	66,860	13,156
70-80	84,731	10,838
80-90	115,518	4,642
90-95	167,249	-5,323
95-99	304,256	-41,778
99-99.9	970,059	-330,898
99.9-99.99	4,927,930	-2,723,656
99.99-top 400	36,044,301	-26,101,983
Top 400 households	456,562,560	-$390,026,495

Sources and Notes: Saez and Zucman, *The Triumph of Injustice*, appendix TC8.

rect for inflation indicates sluggish wage increases, while using a more realistic correction such as the True Living Cost indicates a decline. New means of expropriation out of workers' income after taxes have emerged, as corporations and the wealthy have sought to use every means at their disposal to expand their share of societal income and wealth.

What is clear beyond dispute is that there has been a massive redistribution—money that would previously have gone to workers is now captured by those who are already affluent. A RAND Corporation study examining income distribution from 1975 to 2018 revealed that the highest earners saw their incomes grow much faster than overall economic growth, while those lower on the income ladder experienced progressively smaller gains relative to that growth. During this period, the share of taxable income captured by the top 10 percent of earners jumped from 34 percent to 50 percent of total U.S. personal income, illustrating the extent of this upward transfer of wealth.[75]

The study also estimated that, for the bottom 90 percent, the gap "between what a segment of the population currently earns versus what they would have earned had incomes grown with the broader economy" was approximately $2.5 trillion in 2018. For the entire period from 1975 to 2018, the report estimates that the gap totaled over $47 trillion.

Similarly, economists Emmanuel Saez and Gabriel Zucman found that with equitable income growth from 1980 to 2018, those in the bottom 10 percent of income would have had an income nearly 80 percent greater in 2018 than what they actually received, while median pretax incomes would have been about one-third higher (Table 7.2).[76] Conversely, equitable income growth would have left the richest 400 households with 85 percent *less* income than they received in 2018. They would have needed to scrape by on an average pre-tax income of $66 million instead of $456 million.[77]

The capitalist class has shown itself more than ever to be the ruling class of society. It has been able to pour a huge amount of money into elections and to use its lobbyists to write laws and regulations. The extent and influence of lobbying—mostly in favor of corporations and the wealthy—is considerable, leading to an author of an article in *The Atlantic* to refer to it as "The Real 'Deep State.'"[78] The U.S. Supreme Court, as previously noted, lifted virtually all constraints on campaign contributions by the wealthy, allowing competing sectors of the capitalist class to more effectively buy U.S. elections.

The capitalist class has succeeded in watering down enforcement of many regulations while reducing union membership and suppressing wage gains. As the NAFTA and WTO agreements went into effect in the 1990s, multinational corporations were given greater freedom to invest abroad and repatriate capital at will. The value chains created, where component parts of a commodity are sourced from a variety of countries and companies and assembled in relatively low unit-labor cost regions, have led to gigantic increases in corporate profits.[79] At the same time the conditions of workers in the United States have deteriorated. Many have been left behind, struggling to survive as wages seldom keep up with inflating prices.[80]

The amassing of wealth at the top of society emanates from what is considered "normal" capitalist exploitation, under conditions of "equal exchange" enforced by the labor contract, as well as expropriation (or theft). The combined effect of increases in both exploitation and expropriation in the neoliberal era has been a big squeeze on workers' income. *If the relative shares of various income levels had remained as they were in the 1960s and early '70s, workers—especially those classified as production and non-supervisory workers, comprising approximately 80 percent of the total private workforce—would have had significantly higher income than they now have. The estimated $47 trillion of income "lost" to the bottom 90 percent during the period of 1975–2018 could have helped workers pay for their food, housing, utilities, healthcare, transportation, connectivity, and education while staying out of debt.* And if the government had raised more taxes from the extremely rich, it could have easily created programs and jobs to help people in communities with little hope of a better future. And, of course, if the United States spent less on the military, which accounts for the lion's share of goods and services spending in the federal budget, had fewer military bases abroad, and stopped engaging in foreign wars, significant resources could be freed up for social uses.

The Special Situation of Workers in the Southern United States

The condition of labor in the U.S. South is especially difficult, a legacy of past slavery, current racism, and anti-union sentiment. In the South, wages tend to be low while sales, local, and state taxes on the poorest 20 percent of the population tend to be a much greater percentage of their income than that of the wealthiest one percent. In addition, wage theft is rampant.[81]

The key findings of a 2025 report from the Economic Policy Institute, were:

- Many states across the South use an economic development model that prioritizes the wealthy and corporations at the expense of workers and their families and fosters precarity to maintain racial and class-based hierarchies.
- Southern families face high rates of economic insecurity, and underinvestment in health, childcare, and transportation infrastructure blocks working families from full participation in the economy.
- Southern states have some of the weakest wage theft and paid sick leave laws in the country and are less likely than other states to enforce laws that do exist to protect workers.
- The racist attitudes that inspired discriminatory social welfare programs 90 years ago persist today. These dynamics are especially acute in the South, where the programs are less generous and reach fewer eligible families.
- Many southern lawmakers have repeatedly rejected efforts to expand Medicaid in their states, which has led to thousands of premature deaths and other health and economic consequences. And southern states account for six of the 10 states nationwide with the highest uninsured rates.
- In 11 southern states, the poorest 20% of residents pay more [a higher percent of their income] in sales taxes alone than the top 1% of residents pay in all state and local taxes combined.
- High poverty rates, regressive tax structures, and a failure to tax corporate income mean that southern states collect much

less revenue than other states and are highly dependent on the federal government.

- In recent years, southern states have given away billions of dollars in public revenue in the form of direct subsidies and tax breaks to corporations for projects that often do not benefit communities.[82]

Blame Anyone But Corporations and Capitalists for the Situation

As things have progressed, working people find themselves in increasingly precarious conditions with inadequate income and unpleasant working conditions, leading—especially following the 2021–2022 burst of inflation—to the realization that workers face a general "affordability crisis." Prices for food, healthcare, daycare, rent, electricity, etc., have all increased significantly.

Business interests and the wealthy set out to create conditions more favorable to accumulation of capital as they sought to get a larger portion of the pie. An important part of this effort was the class war waged by capital against workers—a drive against unions and to keep wages from increasing too much. As the robbery continued, and more and more of the income went to the wealthy and less to labor, the effective wages of many workers decreased.

But it is extremely useful to capital to disguise the reality by using a story that distracts attention from the real cause of the problem. One of the ways the system continues to function is by promoting the fiction that it is not business and the wealthy and their influence on government that is causing the difficult conditions of workers. Instead, according to a widely promoted right-wing fantasy, the problems are supposedly migrants taking jobs from citizens and the importing of too many products from abroad (instead of producing them in the United States). While this idea is not new, Trump in 2025 and 2026 is implementing an America First nationalism targeting immigrants with deportations and tariffs against foreign countries. This supposedly will lead to increased goods production in the United States and higher wages. An article in the April 2025 issue of *Bloomberg Businessweek* describes the diversion tactic:

> Broad-based Buy American movements historically reject not only foreign goods but also foreign or non-White workers, even those on US soil. In this way, at least, Buy American campaigns work beautifully: They take existing dissatisfaction and unrest among US workers and reorient it away from those wielding power domestically and toward a foreign threat. Suddenly the most important relationship in the labor economy isn't between workers and owners, but between Americans and their foreign opponents—and big business can more easily cast itself as an ally of the everyman. They'd love to treat their workers well, if only they had the customers to afford to do it.[83]

In addition, the fairy tale that many believe is that your economic condition mainly has to do with you. If you get a good education, make smart decisions, and work hard, you can do well. America is a Horatio Alger story. So, if you are struggling economically or are poor, don't blame the economic system, the wealthy, or the business owners. It's your fault that you have a lousy job or are poor. This false ideology is internalized by both the wealthy at the top and by many of those struggling to make ends meet.

8

Where Things Stand and What Is to Be Done?

THERE IS ONE OVERRIDING REASON why, in a land of such wealth and abundance with huge food supplies and the capacity to rapidly construct housing, many people in the U.S. remain hungry—now called "food insecure"—and homeless. If providing adequate food and housing to everyone were highly profitable, it would happen, because the purpose of investments and economic decision-making in capitalist economies is for companies to reap the highest possible profit.

And what's stopping companies from voluntarily paying a living wage to their workers? Again, it's the single-minded focus on the accumulation of capital and amassing wealth at the top that results in enormous social and environmental consequences: global warming and climate destabilization; soil erosion, deforestation, species extinctions, pollution of air, water, soil, and living organisms; ever-increasing societal inequality with life becoming more unaffordable to workers; unsafe working conditions for many workers; persistence of poverty, hunger, and poor housing even in a society of abundance. Social scientists usually refer to these negative effects as "externalities." However, far from being external to the system of capital, these are the direct results of the way capitalism functions, without internal mechanisms to prevent or mitigate such occurrences/events.

Capitalism is a system in which negative (both unintended as well as intended) consequences abound, and in which wealth accumulates primarily in one sector of society, which then has greater influence over laws and regulations. When there are sufficiently strong countervailing forces, such as a high percentage of workers in militant labor unions, it is possible to have laws and regulations that offer some real protection for workers as well as the environment.

As Harry Magdoff and Paul M. Sweezy explained:

> If a ruling class acquires a monopoly of power and uses it exclusively for its own advantage, the result will be certain disaster. The historical record is replete with such tragedies. What is required for successful political rule, therefore, is either wisdom and self-restraint or counter-pressure from a non-ruling but powerful class or alliance of classes. Whatever may have been true of earlier times, it is pretty clear that no modern capitalist ruling class has ever been blessed with wisdom or self-restraint, from which it follows that such successes as may have been achieved in the way of political rule are the result of effective counter-pressure from other classes.[1]

Through capital's planned and aggressive effort it has, for all practical purposes, acquired a monopoly of power. Capital's campaign to have more control over labor and to secure laws and regulations that allow corporations and the very wealthy to keep more of their income has been successful—*for those at the top*. The "free trade" agreements such as NAFTA and the WTO were put in place as a result of capital's desire to be free to invest and produce abroad with few if any restrictions and to be able to repatriate profits. These agreements were about freeing capital from its geographical restrictions, thereby opening up new profit-making opportunities. What happened to the domestic workforce when production went abroad was of no concern to owners. As more mechanization (now, with robots) coupled with AI comes into use, displaced workers are on their own to deal with the disruptions. And, of course, capital did all it could in other ways to weaken the bargaining position of labor, thus keeping wages from eating into their profits. This did not happen because of some theoretical explanation of economists, though they no doubt assisted in covering up the real goals. It was the use of ruling-class power, mostly unrestrained and unchallenged, that instituted the neoliberal agenda.

The U.S. ruling class has fought hard to acquire a monopoly of power, leading the country and the world into a very dangerous period. The severe ecological, economic, and social problems we face—and the instabilities that accompany these problems—are clear indications of a ruling class that has failed miserably to keep "their" society stable. This failure is the result of a plutocratic monopoly over the reins of both economic and political power used to enhance capital accumulation and inequality. Freedom for a rich oligarchy to operate more or less as they wish leaves the rest of society in a precarious position. The major countervailing force of labor was beaten down while corporate profits soared and the opulent "1 percent" (more accurately 0.001 percent) increased their gigantic pile of riches. It is, of course, not possible to count on the wisdom of capital to solve either the crises in workers' lives or the ecological problems that develop in a highly financialized economy coupled to a co-opted political system.

Joseph Stiglitz, a leftish "new Keynesian" economist, has described the results of neoliberal policies in the United States as allowing "Freedom for the Wolves" to trounce others in society. He then goes on to describe a good society: "A good society . . . must live in harmony with nature. Our current capitalism has made a mess of this. A good society allows individuals to flourish and live up to their potential. In terms of education alone, our current capitalism is failing large portions of the population. A good economic system would encourage people to be honest and empathetic, and foster the ability to cooperate with others. The current capitalist system encourages the antithesis."[2]

His short description of a good society isn't bad. But the "current capitalist system" with which he is so concerned—with the wolves firmly in charge—is a logical outcome of the prolonged stagnation, the rise of financialization, and the class war that capital has waged against workers. Rather than simply seeing the *current incarnation* of capitalism as the problem, it is necessary to trace these disastrous conditions to *the fundamental way in which capitalism functions as a system.*

Workers and unions need to understand that it is not just their boss or supervisor who's causing the problems for labor. Nor is it immigrant labor. Instead, it is capitalism—a system characterized by the accumulation of capital by a small number of capitalists—that is at the heart of the problems we face. A rebuilt union movement is an important goal, but just as important is for it to incorporate an understanding and critique of the capitalist system.

As Bernie Sanders states in the title of his 2024 book, *It's OK to Be Angry About Capitalism.*[3] Given that capital has been engaged in an intensified class war against workers for decades, with disastrous results for all but the wealthy, is it any wonder that workers are now beginning to organize again and to fight back with renewed union struggles? One thing is certain: only a great uprising from below on the scale of the 1930s is capable of producing greater worker power to create a much fairer and more equitable society. While not getting rid of the basic ills of capitalism, a significant increase in the number of workers in militant unions will provide at least some counterweight to the nearly unlimited power of capital. Moreover, this is a necessary step toward transcending the entire inequitable and destructive system of capitalism.

What Harry Magdoff and Paul Sweezy wrote thirty years ago is only more urgent today:

> Now more than ever what is needed is organized, militant struggle to check and reverse capital's onslaught on the earning power and living standards of the world's working and oppressed classes and on the natural environment that is the indispensable foundation for civilized life on an already endangered planet.[4]

The affordability crisis and the intensified exploitation of workers—associated with what we can rightfully call *Grand Theft Capital*—represent capitalism's ongoing war against labor. The solution to these problems is not to return to some imagined better version of capitalism, which never truly existed. Instead, we must move forward toward a fundamentally different kind of society: one that is more equal, more just, and more sustainable, where the free development of each person becomes the basis for the free development of all. In other words, the rational and feasible answer is a *movement toward socialism.*

Notes

Introduction

1. David Leonhardt, "Recent Immigration Surge Has Been Largest in U.S. History," *New York Times*, December 11, 2024.
2. Daniel Singer, *Whose Millennium: Theirs or Ours? (*New York: Monthly Review Press, 1999), 1.
3. Kellen Browning, "Union Leaders Get Tough with Democrats as Members Drift Toward Trump," *New York Times*, August 8, 2025.
4. Shawn Donnan, Nazmul Ahasan, and Alexandre Tanzi, "Economy in Counties Trump Won Points to Governing Challenges," *New York Times*, January 3, 2025.
5. Molly Hennessy-Fiske, "U.S. homelessness surged 18 percent to record level annual report says," *Washington Post*, December 27, 2024; Brian Goldstone, "America Is Pushing Its Workers into Homelessness," *New York Times*, March 1, 2025.
6. Paul Krugman, "Bidenomics Is Still Working Very Well," *New York Times*, February 22, 2024.
7. Catherine Rampell, "How good is the U.S. economy? It's beating pre-pandemic predictions," *Washington Post*, December 8, 2023.
8. Dean Baker, "Why the Public Is So Negative About the Economy," *The Nation*, February 2024.
9. Katherine J. Cramer and Jonathan D. Cohen, "'It's All About Greed and Profit': How Many Americans Feel About the Economy," *New York Times*, February 21, 2024.
10. Ibid.
11. Fred Magdoff and John Bellamy Foster, "The Plight of the U.S. Working Class," *Monthly Review* 65, no. 8 (January 2014): 1–22; Fred Magdoff and John Bellamy Foster, "Grand Theft Capital: The Increasing Exploitation and Robbery of the U.S. Working Class," *Monthly Review* 75, no. 1(May 2023): 1–22.
12. Charlotte Hampton, "Unhappy Workers Cost US Firms $1.9 Trillion," *Bloomberg News*, January 23, 2024.
13. Vanessa Fuhrmans and Lindsay Ellis, "Why Is Everyone So Unhappy at Work Right Now?," *Wall Street Journal*, November 27, 2023.
14. Katherine Bindley, "Tech Workers Are Just Like the Rest of Us: Miserable at Work," *Wall Street* Journal, April 25, 2025.
15. https://www.officialdata.org/inflation-cpi-categories.
16. Klaus Prettner, "Stagnant Wages in the Face of Rising Labor Productivity: The Potential Role of Industrial Robots," *Finance Research Letters* 58, Part D (December 2023): 2.

17. Social Progress Initiative, 2026 Global Social Progress Index, at https://www.socialprogress.org/social-progress-index.
18. Nicholas Kristof, "Life, Liberty and the Pursuit of Unhappiness," *New York Times*, January 14, 2026.
19. Peterson KKF, Health System Tracker, https://www.healthsystem-tracker.org/indicator/health-well-being/life-expectancy/#Life%20expectancy%20at%20birth,%20in%20years,%201980-2022.20.
    David Leonhardt and Ashley Wu, "The U.S. Economy Is Racing Ahead. Almost Everything Else Is Falling Behind," *New York Times*, February 4, 2025.
21. Dexter Filkins, "The U.S. Military's Recruiting Crisis," *The New Yorker*, February 10, 2025.
22. Karl Marx, *Capital*, vol. 1 (London: Penguin, 1976), 914–15; Karl Marx and Frederick Engels, *Collected Works* (New York: International Publishers, 1975), vol. 20, 129.
23. Walter Johnson, "King Cotton's Long Shadow," *New York Times*, March 30, 2013, http://opinionator.blogs.nytimes.com/2013/03/30/king-cottons-long-shadow/.
24. On the role of expropriation in capitalism, including the expropriation of nature, see John Bellamy Foster and Brett Clark, *The Robbery of Nature* (New York: Monthly Review Press, 2020).
25. Maggie Davis and Dan Shepard, "Percentage of Businesses That Fail—And How to Boost Success," April 7, 2025, https://www.lendingtree.com/business/small/failure-rate/.
26. Peter Coy, "Unseparated and Unequal," *New York Times* newsletter, October 17, 2022.
27. Adelle Waldman, "Part-Time Work Has a New, Predatory Logic," *New York Times*, February 20, 2024.
28. Yavor Ivanchev, "Union Power and Worker Welfare," Bureau of Labor Statistics, January 2024.
29. Orlando Mayorquín "Utah Bans Collective Bargaining for Public Workers," *New York Times*, February 15, 2025.
30. Zachary Karabell "Admitting there's no affordability crisis is the first step to solving it," *Washington Post*, January 19, 2026.

1. Overview of U.S. Workers

1. Emphasis added.
2. Jennifer Turner and a team of students and faculty of the Global Human Rights Clinic (GHRC) at the University of Chicago Law School, *Captive Labor: Exploitation of Incarcerated Workers*, ACLU Research Report, June 15, 2022.
3. Caitlin Gilbert, Amanda Morris, and Jacqueline Alemany, "Why

some U.S. disabled workers are making less than a dollar an hour," *Washington Post,* August 30, 2024.

4. Jennifer Calfas and Anthony DeBarros, "U.S. Fertility Rate Falls to Record Low," *Wall Street Journal*, April 25, 2024; Mike Stobbe, "The US fertility rate reached a new low in 2024, CDC data shows," AP, July 24, 2025.
5. Ella Ceron, "From New York to Denver, US Cities Are Seeking Migrants for Jobs," *Bloomberg News*, August 9, 2024.
6. David Leonhardt, "Recent Immigration Surge Has Been Largest in U.S. History," *New York Times*, December 11, 2024.
7. Bureau of Labor Statistics, Establishment Survey Data, Table B-3. Average hourly and weekly earnings of all employees on private non-farm payrolls by industry sector, seasonally adjusted.
8. Joel A. Elvery and Julianne Dunn, "Manufacturing Wage Premiums Have Diverged Between Production and Nonproduction Workers," Federal Reserve Board of Cleveland, Regional Policy Report, November 9, 2021.
9. Lori Aratani, "Generations of workers coveted Boeing jobs. Strike reveals how much has changed," *Washington Post*, September 17, 2024.
10. Ibid.
11. Timothy Kehoe, Kim Ruhl, and Joseph Steinberg, "Global Imbalances and Structural Change in the United States," *Journal of Political Economy* 126/2 (April 2018); Yi Wen and Brian Reinbold, "The U.S. Auto Labor Market since NAFTA," *St. Louis Fed on the Economy*, April 15, 2019.
12. Future of Business, "The Technologies Driving Today's Steel Industry," https://www.futureofbusinessandtech.com/mining-in-america/the-technologies-driving-todays-steel-industry/#:~:text=Gone%20are%20the%20days%20when,mini%2Dmills%20become%20more%20efficient; Schuff Steel, "The Steel Supply Chain: FAQs," https://www.schuff.com/the-steel-supply-chain-faqs/#:~:text=Quarter%203%202021,of%20steel%20was%20around%2010.
13. Kehoe, Ruhl, and Steinberg, "Global Imbalances and Structural Change in the United States."
14. Sebastian Herrera, "Amazon Is on the Cusp of Using More Robots Than Humans in Its Warehouses," *Wall Street Journal,* June 30, 2025.
15. Vanessa Fuhrmans and Lindsay Ellis, "Half of College Grads Are Working Jobs that Don't Use Their Degrees," *Wall Street Journal*, February 22, 2024.
16. Mortiz Altenried, *The Digital Factory* (Chicago: University of Chicago Press, 2022), 3–4; Jennifer Howard, "What Happened to Google's Effort to Scan Millions of University Library Books?," *EdSurge,* August 10, 2017.

17. Gig Economy, Data Hub, "How Many Gig Workers Are There?," https://gigeconomydata.org/basics/how-many-gig-workers-are-there.html.
18. Herrera, "Amazon Is on the Cusp."
19. Chip Cutter and Haley Zimmerman, "CEOs Start Saying the Quiet Part Out Loud: AI Will Wipe Out Jobs," *Wall Street Journal*, July 2, 2025.
20. Kristalina Georgieva, "AI will affect 40% of jobs and probably worsen inequality, says IMF head," *Guardian*, January 15, 2024.
21. Ray A. Smith, "AI Is Starting to Threaten White-Collar Jobs. Few Industries Are Immune," *Wall Street Journal*, February 12, 2024.
22. Heather Long, "Another 'shock' is coming for American jobs," *Washington Post*, April 1, 2025.
23. Danielle Abril, "Labor unions mobilize to challenge advance of algorithms in workplaces," *Washington Post*, August 12, 2025.
24. Cat Zakrzewski and Hannah Natanson, "Silicon Valley's bet on Trump starts to pay off," *Washington Post*, July 24, 2025.
25. Lindsay Ellis and Katherine Bindley, "AI Is Wrecking an Already Fragile Job Market for College Graduates," *Wall Street Journal*, July 29, 2025.
26. Agnee Ghosh and Shirin Ghaffary, "Anthropic Finds Businesses Are Mainly Using AI to Automate Work," *Bloomberg News*, Sept. 15, 2025.
27. Theo Francis, "Behind This Season's Bumper Earnings: Job Cuts, Price Hikes, Glum Workers," *Wall Street Journal*, September 2, 2025.
28. Bureau of Labor Statistics, "Labor Force Characteristics by Race and Ethnicity, 2023," *BLS Reports*, December 2024.
29. BLS reports, Highlights of women's earnings in 2024 (2026), report 1117, January 2026, accessed June 2, 2026 at https://www.bls.gov/opub/reports/womens-earnings/2024/home.htm.
30. U.S. Department of Labor, "Most common occupations for women in the labor force," accessed June 2, 2026 at https://www.statista.com/statistics/1451271/occupations-highest-share-women-world/?srsltid=AfmBOorDZ6xmO1FLNFL94SoQNoIWWOQsq_JKMYBprQH50U5bZemnzOTH
31. Lauren Weber and Stephanie Stamm, "40% of Lawyers Are Women. 7% Are Black. America's Workforce in Charts," Wall Street Journal (Feb. 9, 2024).
32. Brandon Enriquez, "When (government) work disappears: Disparate employment effects of DOGE in the short-run," Economics Letters Vol. 261 (March 2026); Institute for Women's Policy Research (IWPR), "Black Women Disproportionately Sidelined in Year One of Trump's Second Term" (February 10, 2026).

2. The U.S. Ruling Class

1. James Burnham, *The Managerial Revolution* (London: Putnam and Co.,

1941); John Kenneth Galbraith, *American Capitalism: The Concept of Countervailing Power* (Cambridge, MA: Riverside Press, 1952); C. Wright Mills, *The Power Elite* (Oxford: Oxford University Press, 1956), 147–70.

2. C. B. Macpherson, *The Life and Times of Liberal Democracy* (Oxford: Oxford University Press, 1977), 77–92.
3. Mills, *The Power Elite*, 170, 277.
4. G. William Domhoff, "*The Power Elite* and Its Critics," in *C. Wright Mills and The Power Elite*, ed. G. William Domhoff and Hoyt B. Ballard (Boston: Beacon Press, 1968), 276.
5. Nicos Poulantzas, *Political Power and Social Classes* (London: Verso, 1975); Ralph Miliband, *The State in Capitalist Society* (London: Quartet Books, 1969).
6. Paul A. Baran and Paul M. Sweezy, *Monopoly Capital* (New York: Monthly Review Press, 1966), 339.
7. Ibid., 155.
8. Ibid., 108, 336.
9. As shown in Figure 6.2 below, profits per unit of real gross value added (GDP) by U.S nonfinancial corporations dipped only slightly in line with normal business cycle fluctuations in the late 1960s and early 1970s only to bounce back, followed by a long term rise. Moreover, business cycle research has shown that the rise in the wage share of income at the peak of the typical business cycle—emphasized in all theories of a profit squeeze—is not due primarly to the increase in employment income that occurs at this stage, which is at best "tiny," but rather to the fact that "wages are steady, while profit is falling." Howard J. Sherman, *The Roller Coaster Economy* (Armonk, New York: M. E. Sharpe, 2010), 52–53. In general, to speak of a capital shortage restricting investment in a monopoly capitalist economy is fallacious. See Harry Magdoff and Paul M. Sweezy, *The End of Prosperity* (New York: Monthly Review Press, 1977), 91–109.
10. Robert Frank, "Robin Hood in Reverse: The History of a Phrase," CNBC, August 7, 2012.
11. The idea that bailing out troubled companies which took on too much risk will encourage other companies to take excessive risks.
12. Geoff Kabaservice, "The Forever Grievance: Conservatives Have Traded Periodic Revolts for a Permanent Revolution," *Washington Post*, December 4, 2020; Michael Ray, "The Tea Party Movement," *Encyclopedia Britannica*, January 16, 2025, britannica.com; Anthony DiMaggio, *The Rise of the Tea Party: Political Discontent and Corporate Media in the Age of Trump* (New York: Monthly Review Press, 2011).
13. Kabaservice, "The Forever Grievance"; Suzanne Goldenberg, "Tea Party Movement: Billionaire Koch Brothers Who Helped It Grow," *Guardian*,

October 13, 2010; Doug Henwood, "Take Me to Your Leader: The Rot of the American Ruling Class," *Jacobin*, April 27, 2021.

14. On the concept of contradictory class locations, see Erik Olin Wright, *Class, Crisis and the State* (London: Verso, 1978), 74–97; Barbara Ehrenreich, *Fear of Falling: The Inner Life of the Middle Class* (New York: HarperCollins, 1990); Nate Silver, "The Mythology of Trump's 'Working Class' Support," ABC News, May 3, 2016; Thomas Ogorzalek, Spencer Piston, and Luisa Godinez Puig, "White Trump Voters Are Richer than They Appear," *Washington Post*, November 12, 2019.
15. C. Wright Mills, *White Collar* (New York: Oxford University Press, 1953), 353–54.
16. The analysis here is based on John Bellamy Foster, *Trump in the White House* (New York: Monthly Review Press, 2017).
17. Trump quoted in Kabaservice, "The Forever Grievance."
18. Foster, *Trump in the White House*, 26–27.
19. Karl Marx, *Herr Vogt: A Spy in the Worker's Movement* (London: New Park Publications, 1982), 70.
20. Thomas Piketty, *Capital in the Twenty-First Century* (Cambridge, MA: Harvard University Press, 2014), 391–92.
21. Karl Marx, *Herr Vogt: A Spy in the Worker's Movement* (London: New Park Publications, 1982), 70.
22. George Kerevan, "The American Ruling Class Is Shifting Towards Trump," *Brave New Europe*, July 19, 2024, braveneweurope.com.
23. Ibid.; Anna Massoglia, "Outside Spending on 2024 Elections Shatters Records, Fueled by Billion-Dollar Dark Money Infusion,," Open Secrets, November 5, 2024, opensecrets.org.
24. Full Transcript of President Biden's Farewell Address, *New York Times*, January 15, 2025; Bernie Sanders, "The US Has a Ruling Class—And Americans Must Stand Up to It," *Guardian*, September 2, 2022.
25. Dan Alexander and Michela Tindera, "The Net Worth of Joe Biden's Cabinet," *Forbes*, June 29, 2021.
26. Laura Mannweiler, "All the President's Billionaires: The Extraordinary Wealth in Trump's Administration," *U.S. News and World Report*, June 4, 2025; Rick Claypool, "Trump's Billionaire Cabinet Represents the Top 0.0001%," Public Citizen, January 14, 2025, citizen.org; Peter Charalambous, Laura Romero, and Soo Rin Kim, "Trump Has Tapped an Unprecedented 13 Billionaires for his Administration. Here's Who They Are," ABC News, December 17, 2024.
27. Adriana Gomez Licon and Alex Connor, "Billionaires, Tech Titans, Presidents: A Guide to Who Stood Where at Trump's Inauguration," Associated Press, January 21, 2025; Doug Henwood, "Take Me to Your Leader: The Rot of the American Ruling Class," *Jacobin*, April 27, 2021.

28. Bernie Sanders, "The US Has a Ruling Class—And Americans Must Stand Up to It," *Guardian*, September 2, 2022.
29. Bernie Sanders, "Bernie's Statement about the Election," Occupy San Francisco, November 7, 2024, occupysf.net; Jake Johnson, "Sanders Lays Out Plan to Fight Oligarchy as Wealth of Top Billionaires Passes $10 Trillion," *Common Dreams*, December 31, 2024.

3. Monopoly Capital and the Structural Crisis of U.S. Capitalism

1. Harry Magdoff and Paul M. Sweezy, *The Deepening Crisis of U.S. Capitalism* (New York: Monthly Review Press, 1981), 181–82; Harry Magdoff, "International Economic Distress and the Third World," *Monthly Review* 33, no. 11 (April 1982): 3–5.
2. Paul A. Baran and Paul M. Sweezy, *Monopoly Capital* (New York: Monthly Review Press, 1961), 108.
3. John Bellamy Foster, "The Age of Planetary Crisis," *Review of Radical Political Economics* 29, no. 4 (Fall 1997): 116–20.
4. John Bellamy Foster and Fred Magdoff, *The Great Financial Crisis* (New York: Monthly Review Press, 2009), 63–76.
5. Christopher Mims, "Why There Are More Consumer Goods Than Ever," *Wall Street Journal*, April 25, 2016.
6. Calculated from St. Louis Federal Reserve FRED, "Real Gross Domestic Product Billions of Chained 2012 Dollars Quarterly Seasonally Adjusted Annual Rate" (data series GDPC1).
7. Harry Magdoff and Paul M. Sweezy, *Stagnation and the Financial Explosion* (New York: Monthly Review Press, 1986); Harry Magdoff and Paul M. Sweezy, *The Irreversible Crisis* (New York: Monthly Review Press, 1987); John Bellamy Foster and Robert W. McChesney, *The Endless Crisis: How Monopoly-Finance Capital Produces Stagnation and Upheaval from the USA to China* (New York: Monthly Review Press, 2012).
8. Eric Roston, "Disaster Recovery Is Big Business," Bloomberg News, October 21, 2025.

4. The Financialization of the Economy

1. Foster and Magdoff, *The Great Financial Crisis*, 63–76. In a single week in March 2023 the Federal Reserve bailed out collapsing banks, Silicon Valley oligarchs, and venture capital firms to the tune of $300 billion. See Ben Norton, "US Government Bailout of Silicon Valley Banks Is $300 Billion Gift to Rich Oligarchs," *Geopolitical Economy*, March 19, 2023, geopoliticaleconomy.com.
2. Bethany McLean, "Senate Report: How private equity 'gutted' dozens of U.S. hospitals," *Washington Post*, October 17, 2024.

3. Alexandra Heal, "Carried interest: Private equity's tax break," *Financial Times,* October 27, 2024.
4. Mike Baker, Maureen Farrell, and Serge F. Kovaleski, "As Wall Street Chases Profits, Fire Departments Have Paid the Price," *New York Times*, February 17, 2025. Emphasis added.
5. Chris Cumming, "State Legislatures Enact Laws to Curtail Healthcare Dealmaking," *Wall Street Journal*, April 19, 2024.
6. Harriet Agnew, "Hedge fund managers pocket nearly half of investment gains as fees," *Financial Times*, January 19, 2025.
7. Lina Khan and Sandeep Vaheesan, "Market Power and Inequality: The Antitrust Counterrevolution and Its Discontents," *Harvard Law and Policy Review* 11, no. 1 (2017): 235–94.
8. John Bellamy Foster, Robert W. McChesney, and R. Jamil Jonna, "Monopoly and Competition in Twenty-First Century Capitalism," *Monthly Review* 62, no. 11 (April 2011): 6–7.
9. Barry Bluestone and Bennett Harrison, *The Deindustrialization of America: Plant Closings, Community Abandonment, and the Dismantling of Basic Industry* (New York: Basic Books, 1982).
10. Adrian Wooldridge, "How Has the 21st Century Gone So Wrong?," *Bloomberg News,* December 30, 2024.
11. See John Bellamy Foster, R. Jamil Jonna, and Brett Clark, "The Contagion of Capital," *Monthly Review* 72, no. 8 (January 2021): 4–5.
12. John Bellamy Foster, "Absolute Capitalism," *Monthly Review* 71, no. 1 (May 2019): 1–13.
13. Calculated from Bureau of Economic Analysis NIPA Tables 6.16A through 6.16D, Corporate Profits by Industry.
14. Andrew Ross Sorkin, "The Rules of Investing Are Being Loosened: Could It Lead to the Next 1929?," *New York Times*, October 13, 2025.
15. Allison Herren Lee, "Going Dark: The Growth of Private Markets and the Impact on Investors and the Economy," Remarks at the SEC Speaks in 2021, October 12, 2021, sec.gov.
16. Paul Caruana Galizia and Chris Cook, "Black applicants twice as likely to be rejected for a US mortgage," *Financial Times*, September 4, 2025.
17. Gisela Cernadas and John Bellamy Foster, "Actual U.S. Military Spending Reached $1.537 Trillion in 2022—More than Twice Acknowledged Level: New Estimates Based on U.S. National Accounts," *Monthly Review* 75, no. 6 (November 2023); John Bellamy Foster, Hannah Holleman, and Robert W. Chesney, "The U.S. Imperial Triangle and Military Spending," *Monthly Review* 60, no. 5 (October 2008): 1–19.
18. Peter G. Peterson Foundation, "U.S. Spends More on Defense than the Next 9 Countries Combined," update May 5, 2025, https://www.pgpf.

org/article/the-united-states-spends-more-on-defense-than-the-next-9-countries-combined/.

19. Bernd Debusmann Jr., "Trump Seeks $1.5tn for Defence Alongside Domestic Spending Cuts," *BBC News*, April 3, 2026.
20. Karl Marx, *Capital*, vol. 1 (London: Penguin, 1976), 919.
21. Magdoff and Sweezy, *Stagnation and the Financial Explosion*; Magdoff and Sweezy, *The Irreversible Crisis.*
22. Oren Cass, "The Finance Industry Is a Grift. Let's Start Treating It That Way," *New York Times*, February 6, 2026.

5. Capital Fights for an Even Larger Slice of the Pie

1. For example, see Charles V. Bagli, "A Trump Empire Built on Inside Connections and $885 Million in Tax Breaks," *New York Times*, September 17, 2016.
2. "Unchecked Corporate Pricing Power Is a Factor in US Inflation," *Financial Times*, March 18, 2023.
3. Leo Huberman, *The Labor Spy Racket* (Modern Age Books, 1937, republished by Monthly Review Press in 1966).
4. David Montgomery, *The Fall of the House of Labor* (Cambridge: Cambridge University Press, 1987), 464.
5. David Milton, *The Politics of U.S. Labor: From the Great Depression to the New Deal* (New York: Monthly Review Press, 1982).
6. Lewis F. Powell, Jr., "Attack On American Free Enterprise System," August 23, 1971, accessible at https://www.reuters.com/investigates/special-report/assets/usa-courts-secrecy-lobbyist/powell-memo.pdf.
7. U.S. Chamber of Commerce Editorial, "Changing of the Business Guard, Nation's *Business Magazine, August*," 85: 68–69 (August 1997).
8. William Simon, *A Time for Action*, back cover, https://www.ebay.com
9. For a comprehensive history of business's assault on labor over the past half-century, see David N. Gibbs *Revolt of the Rich: How the Politics of the 1970s Widened America's Class Divide* (New York: Columbia University Press, 2024).
10. Cited in David M. Gordon, "Recession Is Capitalism as Usual," *New York Times*, April 27, 1975.
11. Cited in Harry Magdoff and Paul Sweezy, "The Economic Crisis in Historical Perspective—Part II," *Monthly Review* vol. 26, no. 11 (April 1975). Emphasis added.
12. Simon, *A Time for Action.*
13. Harry Magdoff, Special Collections, University of Pittsburgh Johnstown Library, Manuscript Group 176, Dr. James Dougherty Collection, Series 7, Box 1–3, Paul Sweezy and Harry Magdoff, November 23, 1983 (VHS).

14. Calculated from "Annual Work Stoppages Involving 1000 or More Workers 1947–Present," Bureau of Economic Analysis.
15. Ronda Kaysen and Robert Gebeloff, "Where Did All the American-Born Roofers Go?," *New York Times,* January 14, 2026.
16. Steven Greenhouse, "'Old-School Union Busting': How US Corpora-tions Are Quashing the New Wave of Organizing," *Guardian*, February 26, 2023.
17. Celine McNicholas, Marc Edayadi, Daniel Perez, Margaret Poydock, and Ben Zipperer, "Employers Are Charged with Violating Federal Law in Nearly 40% of Union Elections," *Working Economics* (blog), Economic Policy Institute, posted February 3, 2023, epi.org.
18. Noam Scheiber, "Amazon Says Labor Board Violates the U.S. Constitution," *New York Times*, February 17, 2023.
19. Konrad Putzier and Lauren Weber, "Balance of Power Shifts Back Toward Bosses," *Wall Street Journal,* January 13, 2025.
20. Laura Feiveson, "Labor Unions and the U.S. Economy," U.S. Dept. of Treasury featured news story, August 28, 2023, https://home.treasury.gov/news/featured-stories/labor-unions-and-the-us-economy.
21. The share of federal taxes that corporations pay has declined from nearly 40 percent in 1950 to around 10 to 15 percent in 2023. This means that personal income taxes need to take up the slack, going from about 50 percent of federal tax receipts in 1950 to around 80 percent in 2023. This, of course, puts more pressure on working people receiving modest incomes.
22. Ben Stein, "In Class Warfare, Guess Which Class Is Winning," *New York Times*, November 26, 2006.
23. Hamilton Nolan, "Class War in America," *How Things Work* website, July 3, 2023, at https://www.hamiltonnolan.com/p/class-war-usa?utm_source= publication-search.
24. Michael Sainato, "'We Will Figure Out How to Fire You': How Corporate America Is Hitting Back Against Unions," *Guardian*, January 31, 2023.
25. Franklin Foer, "The Real 'Deep State,'" *The Atlantic*, July/August 2024.
26. Pew Research Center, *Americans' Dismal View of the Nation's Politics* (2023),www.pewresearch.org/wp-content/uploads/sites/20/2023/09/PP_2023.09.19_views-of-politics_REPORT.pdf
27. Claire Cain Miller, "How Some Voters Moved from Bernie Sanders to Donald Trump," *New York Times*, December 8, 2024.
28. Martin Gilens and Benjamin Page, "Testing Theories of American Politics: Elites, Interest Groups, and Average Citizens," *Perspectives on Politics* 12/3 (September 2014): 564–81.
29. Jeffrey M. Jones, "U.S. Perceptions of 'Fair' Income Taxes Hold Near Record Low," Gallop News, April 8, 2025, https://news.gallup.com/

poll/659003/perceptions-fair-income-taxes-hold-near-record-low.aspx?utm_source=substack&utm_medium=email.

30. Michael Sainato, "'A literal gut punch': Missouri workers devastated by Republican repeal of paid sick leave," *Guardian*, August 12, 2025.
31. Keneth Vogel and David Yaffee-Bellany, "Donor List Suggests Scale of Trump's Pay-for-Access Operation," *New York Times*, August 3, 2025.
32. Filippo Lancieri, Eric A. Posner, and Luigi Zingales, "The Political Economy of the Decline of Antitrust Enforcement in the United States," NBER Working Paper No. 30326 (August 2022). https://www.nber.org/system/files/working_papers/w30326/w30326.pdf
33. Ibid.
34. Ibid.
35. John Bellamy Foster, Robert W. McChesney, and Jamill Jonna, "Monopoly and Competition in 21st Century Capitalism," *Monthly Review* 62, no. 11 (April 2011): 6–11. Spencer Y. Kwon, Yueran Ma, and Kaspar Zimmermann, "100 Years of Rising Corporate Concentration," Becker Friedman Institute for Economics, University of Chicago, April 5 2023.
36. Brooke Masters, "The Boss Is Back." *Financial Times*, August 18, 2025.
37. Chip Cutter, "CEOs Are Shrinking Their Workforces—And They Couldn't Be Prouder," *Wall Street Journal*, July 27, 2025.
38. Ibid.
39. Paul Krugman, "The Economics of Smoot Hawley 2.0, Part II," Substack, August 10, 2025.

6. Grand Theft Capital and the Origins of the New Billionaire Economy

1. Michael Smolyansky, "End of an Era: The Coming Long-Run Slowdown in Corporate Profit Growth and Stock Returns," Finance and Economics Discussion Series (FEDS) of the Federal Reserve System, June 2023, https://www.federalreserve.gov/econres/feds/end-of-an-era-the-coming-long-run-slowdown-in-corporate-profit-growth-and-stock-returns.
2. Calculated as 10-yr moving averages from Table 1.14, "Gross Value Added of Domestic Corporate Business," FRED Database St. Louis Federal Reserve.
3. Michael Mazerov, "Policy Brief: States Can Fight Corporate Tax Avoidance by Requiring Worldwide Combined Reporting," Center on Budget and Policy Priorities, March 29, 2024.
4. Thomas Tørsløv, Ludvig Wier, and Gabriel Zucman, "The Missing Profits of Nations," *Review of Economic Studies* 90 (3) (2022).
5. Jan De Loecker, Jan Eeckhout, and Gabriel Unger, "The Rise of Market Power and the Macroeconomic Implications," *Quarterly Journal of Economics* 135/2 (2020).
6. Isabella M. Weber and Evan Wasner, "Seller's Inflation, Profits, and

Conflict: Why Can Large Firms Hike Prices in an Emergency?," *Review of Keynesian Economics* 11, no. 2 (Summer 2023): 183–213.

7. Kathryn Edwards, "Corporate America's New Slogan: Make More, Pay Less," *Bloomberg News*, February 23, 2026.
8. Sophie Alexander, "Private Jets and Car Washes Are the Latest Tax Shields for the Ultrarich," *Bloomberg News*, October 27, 2025.
9. Adam Lowenstein, "Trump Gave Top US Firms Staggering Tax Cuts, with Some Paying $0 or Less," *Guardian*, February 29, 2024.
10. Statista Research Department, "U.S. CEO-to-worker compensation ratio of top firms 1965–2022," accessed June 8, 2024, https://www.statista.com/statistics/261463/ceo-to-worker-compensation-ratio-of-top-firms-in-the-us/#:~:text=In%202022%2C%20it%20was%20estimated,key%20industry%20of%20their%20firm.
11. Jeff Sommer, "A New Measure Shows C.E.O. Pay at Even More Astronomical Levels," *New York Times*, June 7, 2024.
12. Annie Lowrey, "How the Richest People in America Avoid Paying Taxes," *The Atlantic*, August 25, 2025.
13. Calculated from U.S. Department of the Treasury, "Federal Revenue Trends Over Time, Fiscal Years 2015–2022, Inflation Adjusted—2022 Dollars," chart, September 30, 2022, fiscaldata.treasury.gov.
14. Ashlea Ebeling and Richard Rubin, "IRS Targets Wealthy Non-Filers," *Wall Street Journal*, March 1, 2024.
15. Evan Osnos, "The Getty Family's Trust Issues," *The New Yorker*, January 23, 2023.
16. Rachel Louise Ensign, "The U.S. Economy Depends More Than Ever on Rich People," *Wall Street Journal*, February 23, 2025; Jonnelle Marte, "Top 10% of Earners Drive a Growing Share of US Consumer Spending," *Bloomberg News*, September 16, 2025.

7. The Affordability Crisis of the Working Class

1. Barbara Ehrenreich, *Nickel and Dimed* (New York: Metropolitan Books, 2001), 221.
2. Fred Magdoff and Harry Magdoff, "Disposable Workers: Today's Reserve Army of Labor," *Monthly Review* 55, no. 11 (April 2004): 18–35.
3. Nicholas Megaw, "US companies say it is easier to hire despite low jobless rate," *Financial Times*, February 26, 2023.
4. John Bellamy Foster and Robert W. McChesney, *The Endless Crisis* (New York: Monthly Review Press, 2012), 144–47.
5. St. Louis Federal Reserve FRED Database, "Median Household Income in the United States," (MEHOINUSA646N).
6. Ben Casselman and Conor Dougherty, "Want a House Like This? Prepare for a Bidding War with Investors," *New York Times*, June 20, 2019.

7. Will Parker, "Wall Street Has Spent Billions Buying Homes. A Crackdown Is Looming," *Wall Street Journal*, April 29, 2024.
8. Rebecca Picciotto, "Wall Street Is Betting Billions on Rental Homes as Ownership Slips Out of Reach," *Wall Street Journal*, December 10, 2024.
9. Benjamin Oreskes, "Hochul Seeks to Limit Private-Equity Ownership of Homes in New York," *New York Times*, January 9, 2025.
10. Augusta Saraiva, "Foreigners Are Buying US Homes Again While Americans Get Sidelined," *Bloomberg Businessweek*, August 18, 2025.
11. Jedidajah Otte, "'I feel trapped': How home ownership has become a nightmare for many Americans," *Guardian*, February 24, 2025.
12. Metropolitan Area Planning Council, "Homes for Profit: Speculation and Investment in Greater Boston," https://homesforprofit.mapc.org/report.
13. Emily Badger, "Whatever Happened to the Starter Home?," *New York Times*, September 23, 2023.
14. Carol Ryan, "The U.S. Has More Fancy Apartments Than It Is Able to Fill," *Wall Street Journal*, January 10, 2025.
15. Lauren Aratani, "American Dream of Owning a Home Is Dead Majority of Renters Say," *Bloomberg News*, March 12, 2024.
16. Ken Sweet and Cora Lewis, "Renters Use 'Rent Now, Pay Later' Services to Manage Monthly Payments, but Fees Raise Concerns," AP, February 4, 2026.
17. Anna Bahney, "The US housing market is short 6.5 million homes," CNN, March 8, 2023.
18. Laura Bliss and Klara Auerbach, "Why Access to Running Water Is a Luxury in Wealthy US Cities," *Bloomberg News*, July 17, 2025.
19. National Multifamily Housing Council website, https://www.nmhc.org/research-insight/the-nmhc-50/top-50-lists/2023-top-developers-list/?utm_source=substack&utm_medium=email.
20. Eric Lynch, "Top 10 Builder Share Jumps in 2022," National Association of Home Builders, https://eyeonhousing.org/2023/06/top-10-builder-share-jumps-in-2022.
21. Kaysen and Gebeloff, "Where Did All the American-Born Roofers Go?"
22. Kirsty Lang, "Lessons from Vienna: A Housing Success Story 100 Years in the Making," *Financial Times*, December 30, 2022; Thomas Fuller, "How Does Paris Stay Paris? By Pouring Billions Into Public Housing," *New York Times*, March 17, 2024.
23. AAA, https://www.aaa.com/autorepair/articles/average-annual-cost-of-new-vehicle-ownership; Ann Carnes, "The Rising Costs of Owning a Car," *New York Times*, September 23, 2023.
24. Jade Thomas and Keith Naughton, "Cars Are So Expensive That Buyers Need Seven-Year Loans," *Bloomberg News*, August 25, 2025.

25. Paulina Cachero and Paige Smith, "Americans Are Racking Up 'Phantom Debt' That Wall Street Can't Track," *Bloomberg*, May 7, 2024.
26. Ben Holland. "Americans Now Pay as Much Interest on Other Debt as on Mortgages," *Bloomberg News*, March 5, 2024.
27. Jessica Grose, "What American Families Experienced Is Not Something That You Get Over," *New York Times*, March 13, 2024.
28. Erum Salam, "Nearly 50% of US parents financially supporting adult children, study finds," *Bloomberg News*, March 12, 2024.
29. Lauren Cohen, Umit Gurun, and N. Bugra Ozel, "Too Many Managers: The Strategic Use of Titles to Avoid Overtime Payments," NBER Working Paper no. 30826, nber.org.
30. Hannah Dreier, "Alone and Exploited, Migrant Children Work Brutal Jobs Across the U.S.," *New York Times*, February 25, 2023, updated February 28, 2023.
31. Nina Mast, "Child labor remains a key state legislative issue in 2024," Economic Policy Institute, February 7, 2024, https://www.epi.org/blog/child-labor-remains-a-key-state-legislative-issue-in-2024-state-lawmakers-must-seize-opportunities-to-strengthen-standards-resist-ongoing-attacks-on-child-labor-laws/.
32. Noam Scheiber, "U.S. Moves to Bar Noncompete Agreements in Labor Contracts," *New York Times*, January 6, 2023.
33. Zachary Mider, "Giving Four Months' Notice or Paying to Quit Has These Workers Feeling Trapped," *Bloomberg Businessweek*, January 30, 2023.
34. Office of the Minnesota Attorney General, "Wage Theft," ag.state.mn.us.
35. Lisa Rowan and Korrena Bailie, "How to Spot Wage Theft and What to Do If It Happens to You," *Forbes Advisor*, February 2, 2022.
36. U.S. Dept. of Labor, "Department of Labor finds poultry processor illegally endangered children in dangerous jobs, robbed workers of wages, retaliated by firing workers," press release, December 4, 2023, https://www.dol.gov/newsroom/releases/whd/whd20231204.
37. Josh Funk, "US Rail Industry Defends Safety Record amid Staffing Cuts," AP News, May 16, 2021.
38. Ibid.
39. Michael Sainato, "Railroad workers pressure Congress and Biden to address working conditions," *Guardian*, December 16, 2022.
40. Michael Sainato, "Ohio Train Derailment Reveals Need for Urgent Reform, Workers Say," *Guardian*, February 23, 2023. See also Michael Sainato, "US Rail Workers Told to Skip Inspections as Questions Mount Over Ohio Crash," *Guardian*, March 3, 2023.
41. Intan Suwandi, R. Jamil Jonna, and John Bellamy Foster, "Global Commodity Chains and the New Imperialism," *Monthly Review* 70, no. 10 (March 2019): 1–24. See also Intan Suwandi, *Value Chains* (New

York: Monthly Review Press, 2019).

42. Anne Case and Angus Deaton, *Deaths of Despair and the Future of Capitalism* (Princeton: Princeton University Press, 2021).
43. Matthew Desmond, "Why Poverty Persists in America," *New York Times Magazine*, March 12, 2023.
44. Elijah Nicholson-Messmer and Ella Ceron, "Bitcoin ATMs Flood Black, Latino Areas, Charging Fees up to 22%," *Bloomberg News*, April 17, 2024; Dedrick Asante-Muhammad, "Bitcoin ATMs reprise a painful history in finance," *Financial Times*, September 5, 2025.
45. Hilary Beaumont, "Climate Change Driving Demand for Predatory Loans, Research Shows," *Guardian*, April 15, 2024.
46. AFL-CIO, "Death on the Job: The Toll of Neglect," 31st ed. (April 2022), https://aflcio.org/sites/default/files/2022-04/2214_DOTJ_Final_42622_nobug.pdf.
47. Noam Scheiber, "Amazon Disregarded Internal Warnings on Injuries, Senate Investigation Claims," *New York Times*, December 16, 2024.
48. AFL-CIO, "Death on the Job: The Toll of Neglect."
49. Ronda Kaysen, "A Construction Worker's Suicide Highlights a Wider Crisis," *New York Times*, January 8, 2026.
50. Todd Frankel, "It was the Deadliest Workplace in America. So Why Didn't Safety Regulators Shut It Down?," *Washington Post*, February 16, 2025.
51. Nina Lakhanim, "'You Feel Like You're Suffocating': Florida Outdoor Workers Are Collapsing in the Heat Without Water and Shade," *Guardian*, August 14, 2024.
52. Environmental Protection Agency, "A Closer Look: Heat-Related Workplace Deaths" (2024), https://www.epa.gov/climate-indicators/closer-look-heat-related-workplace-deaths#:~:text=Feature%20%7C%20Technical%20Documentation-,Key%20Points,reported%20data%20(Figure%201).
53. Juley Fulcher, "Scorched States: A Report Card on State Laws Protecting Workers from Heat," *Public Citizen* (May 22, 2024).
54. Kate Morgan, "In Appalachia, a Father Got Black Lung. Then His Son Did, Too," *New York Times*, June 19, 2025.
55. Hannah Dreier, "Wildfire Fighters Unmasked in Toxic Smoke Are Getting Sick and Dying," *New York Times*, August 17, 2025.
56. Alight, "Alight Study Reveals Employee Wellbeing Has Plateaued and Trust in Employer Efforts Has Eroded," September 19, 2023, https://investor.alight.com/news/news-details/2023/Alight-Study-Reveals-Employee-Wellbeing-Has-Plateaued-and-Trust-in-Employer-Efforts-Has-Eroded/default.aspx.
57. Noah Weiland, "As Medicaid Shrinks, Clinics for the Poor Are Trying to Survive," *New York Times*, February 24, 2024.

58. Peter Goodman, "The Real Reason Americans Worry About Trade," *New York Times*, August 25, 2025.
59. Editorial Board, "A Better Form of Capitalism Is Possible," *Financial Times*, December 30, 2020.
60. Average compensation (or wage) will be higher than median values when there are some high earners in a group of mostly low earners.
61. Laura Bliss and Klara Auerbach, "Inflation Is Worse Than the CPI Shows, Says Ex US Comptroller," *Bloomberg*, September 22, 2025.
62. Laura Bliss and Klara Auerbach, "Are US Statistics Understating Inflation?," *Bloomberg Businessweek*, October 2025.
63. Avik Roy, "Summers: Inflation Reached 18% in 2022 Using the Government's Previous Formula," *Forbes*, March 23, 2024.
64. Kevin Kelleher, "U.S. Corporations Are Hoarding More and More Cash Overseas," *Fortune*, August 3, 2022; Alexandra Scaggs, "Companies' confusing cash hoards: Why Aren't They Getting Spent?," *Financial Times*, November 16, 2023. For a detailed explanation of the conditions leading to corporate cash hoarding, see John Bellamy Foster, R. Jamil Jonna, and Brett Clark, "The Contagion of Capital," *Monthly Review* 72, no. 8 (February 2021): 1–19; Financial Accounts of the United States — Z.1, L.103 Nonfinancial Corporate Business.
65. Dan Gallagher, "Big Tech Has a Big Cash Problem," *Wall Street Journal*, April 7, 2024.
66. U.S. Census Bureau, Quarterly Financial Report: "U.S. Corporations: All Manufacturing: Total Cash on Hand and in U.S. Banks," [QFRTCASHMFGUSNO], retrieved from FRED, Federal Reserve Bank of St. Louis, https://fred.stlouisfed.org/series/QFRTCASHMFGUSNO, January 15, 2026.
67. Hannah Miao, "Corporate Stock Buybacks Help Keep Market Afloat," *Wall Street Journal*, February 27, 2023; PR Newsletter, "S&P 500 Q4 2023 Buybacks Increase 18.0% Compared to Q3, Full Year 2023 Shows Decline of 13.8% from 2022 Levels, Earnings Per Share Impact Continues to Decline; Buybacks Tax Reduced Q4 Operating Earnings by 0.44% and 2023 by 0.40%," https://www.prnewswire.com/news-releases/sp-500-q4-2023-buybacks-increase-18-0-compared-to-q3--full-year-2023-shows-decline-of-13-8-from-2022-levels-earnings-per-share-impact-continues-to-decline-buybacks-tax-reduced-q4-operating-earnings-by-0-44-and-2023-by-0-40-302091498.html.
68. William Janeway, "What Will Remain After the AI and Crypto Bubbles?," *Project Syndicate*, August 29, 2025, https://www.project-syndicate.org.
69. Lex (Opinion), "Venture capital dry powder has nowhere to go," *Financial Times*, April 12, 2024.

70. Manhattan Institute, "Cost-of-Thriving Index: Reevaluating the Prosperity of the American Family," https://manhattan.institute/article/the-cost-of-thriving-index-reevaluating-the-prosperity-of-the-american-family; Oren Cass, "The 2023 Cost-of-Thriving Index: Tracking the Catastrophic Erosion of Middle-Class Life in America," americancompass.org.
71. Alexandre Tanzi, "Even on $100,000-Plus, More Americans Are Living Paycheck to Paycheck," *Bloomberg News*, January 30, 2023.
72. Brittany King, "Those Who Married Once More Likely Than Others to Have Retirement Savings," U.S. Census Bureau, https://www.census.gov/library/stories/2022/01/women-more-likely-than-men-to-have-no-retirement-savings.html.
73. Barbara A. Butrica, Howard M. Iams, Karen E. Smith, and Eric J. Toder, "The Disappearing Defined Benefit Pension and Its Potential Impact on the Retirement Incomes of Baby Boomers," Social Security Bulletin 69, no. 3, 2009, https://www.bls.gov/opub/ted/2024/15-percent -of-private -industry-workers-had-access-to-a-defined-benefit-retirement-plan.htm.
74. Prettner, "Stagnant Wages in the Face of Rising Labor Productivity," 2.
75. Carter C. Price and Kathryn A. Edwards, "Trends in Income from 1975 to 2018," RAND Corporation Working Paper WR-A156-1, Santa Monica, 2020, 12, 40.
76. Emmanuel Saez and Gabriel Zucman, "The Rise of Income and Wealth Inequality in America: Evidence from Distributional Macroeconomic Accounts," *Journal of Economic Perspectives* 34, no. 4 (Fall 2020): 3–26.
77. Saez and Zucman, "The Rise of Income and Wealth Inequality in America"; Emmanuel Saez and Gabriel Zucman, *Triumph of Injustice: How the Rich Dodge Taxes and How to Make Them Pay* (New York: W. W. Norton, 2019), appendixTC8.
78. Franklin Foer, "The Real 'Deep State,'" *The Atlantic*, July/August 2024.
79. Suwandi, *Value Chains*; John Smith, *Imperialism in the Twenty-First Century* (New York: Monthly Review Press, 2016).
80. The COVID-19 pandemic set off a sellers' inflation in the United States and other countries where monopolistic firms, initially raising prices in relation to supply chain breakdown, have continued to increase their markups and prices, generating record profit margins. See Isabella M. Weber and Evan Wasner, "Sellers' Inflation, Profits, and Conflict: Why Can Large Firms Hike Prices in an Emergency?," Political Economy Research Institute, Working Paper Series, no. 571, University of Massachusetts Amherst, February 2023, peri.umass.edu; Financial Times Visual and Data Interpretation Team, "Unchecked Corporate Pricing Power Is a Factor in US Inflation," *Financial Times*, March 19, 2023.
81. Nina Mast, "How Anti-Worker Policies, Crony Capitalism, and

Privatization Keep the South Locked Out of Shared Prosperity," Rooted in Racism and Economic Exploitation: Part Five, Economic Policy Institute, June 18, 2025.

82. Ibid.
83. Amanda Mull, "The Real Reason Trump Is Pushing 'Buy American'," *Businessweek*, April 2025.

8. Where Things Stand and What Is to Be Done?

1. Harry Magdoff and Paul M. Sweezy, "The Political Tragedy of Capitalist Rule," *Monthly Review* 75, no. 1 (May 2023): 61–62.
2. Joseph Stiglitz, "Freedom for the Wolves," *The Atlantic*, https://www.theatlantic.com/ideas/archive/2024/04/neoliberalism-freedom-markets-hayek/678124/.
3. Bernie Sanders, *It's OK to Be Angry About Capitalism* (New York: Crown, 2023).
4. Magdoff and Sweezy, "The Political Tragedy of Capitalist Rule."

Index